PERSONAL FREEDOM
&
CIVIC DUTY ™

UNDERSTANDING YOUR
RIGHT TO FREEDOM
FROM SEARCHES

BRIAN CARSON AND
CATHERINE RAMEN

ROSEN
PUBLISHING®

New York

Published in 2012 by The Rosen Publishing Group, Inc.
29 East 21st Street, New York, NY 10010

Library of Congress Cataloging-in-Publication Data

Carson, Brian.
Understanding your right to freedom from searches/
Brian Carson, Catherine Ramen.—1st ed.
    p. cm.—(Personal freedom and civic duty)
Includes bibliographical references and index.
ISBN 978-1-4488-4670-2 (library binding)
1. Privacy, right of—United States—Juvenile literature.
2. Searches and seizures—United States—Juvenile literature.
3. United States. Constitution. 4th Amendment—Juvenile
literature. I. Ramen, Catherine. II. Title.
JC596.2.U5C38 2012
323.44'8—dc22
                                          2010044135

Manufactured in the United States of America

CPSIA Compliance Information: Batch #S11YA: For further information, contact Rosen Publishing, New York, New York, at 1-800-237-9932.

On the cover: A man is searched by police in New York City's Times Square as part of a routine counterterrorist domestic security effort.

CONTENTS

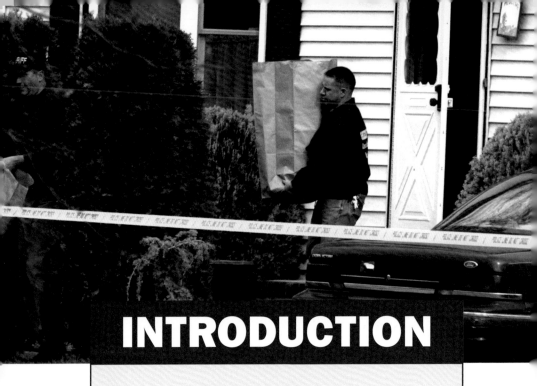

INTRODUCTION

In April 2010, police officers from the Greene County Sheriff's Department descended upon Central High School in Springfield, Missouri. They were there for one of five annual "lockdowns" of the school. During these lockdowns, students were confined to classrooms or the library while police officers, with the help of drug-sniffing dogs, searched the contents of lockers, including backpacks, for illegal drugs. The sheriff's department considered these lockdowns "standard drills."

Yet two of the students whose bags and lockers were searched—and in which nothing illegal was

Above: Police remove evidence from the Toms River, New Jersey, home of a police officer suspected of having killed five of his neighbors and wounding his own police chief.

found—were the children of a Springfield city council-man, Doug Burlison. He and his wife, Mellony, were outraged by what they considered an unwarranted search of their children's personal possessions and an invasion of their privacy. They soon announced their intention to sue Springfield's school system, its super-intendent, Central High's principal, and the Greene County sheriff. The Burlisons claimed that the rights of all students at Central High were violated by these lockdowns, particularly their Fourth Amendment rights, which protect American citizens against unreasonable search and seizure.

The first ten amendments to the U.S. Constitution, known collectively as the Bill of Rights, center upon individual and states' rights. The text of the Fourth Amendment reads:

> *The right of the people to be secure in their persons, houses, papers, and effects, against unreasonable searches and seizures, shall not be violated, and no Warrants shall issue, but upon probable cause, supported by Oath or affirmation, and particularly describing the place to be searched, and the persons or things to be seized.*

In the case of the Central High lockdowns, there was no probable cause (the officers weren't acting upon a specific tip that a particular student or group of students possessed drugs that were stashed in the school) and the sheriff's department presented no search warrant detailing precisely whom they wished to search and exactly what they were searching for. Instead, as part of a regular program of sweeps, the police engaged in a broad and indiscriminate examination of all students' private possessions, without a warrant, a specific target or sought-for item, or any immediately compelling reason to engage in the search.

According to Jason Umbarger, the attorney who filed the case on behalf of the Burlisons, "Warrentless mass searches of high school students send a horrific message, teach a horrific message, to the high school students of our community that they're powerless against the state, against the police" (as quoted by Doug Magditch, reporting for KSPR, the local ABC television affiliate). "Students do not leave their constitutional rights at the school house gates." Yet the attorney for the Springfield public school system counters that, unlike the probable cause required when law enforcement officials wish to search an adult, "school officials do not have to have probable cause for a search; they have to have reasonable suspicion," a far lower standard of justification. The Greene County sheriff, Jim Arnott, agrees, saying his department acted within the requirements of state and federal law.

Ultimately, this case will be decided—perhaps years from now—by a state and/or federal court and may even reach the Supreme Court, the ultimate arbiter of constitutional issues and the rights of citizens versus the powers of the government.

The U.S. Constitution is one of the world's most remarkable and inspiring documents. In simple, clear language, it manages not only to safeguard the liberty of the people of the United States, but at the time of its drafting and ratification in 1787–1788, it also created a bold new plan to fundamentally change the relationship between the government and the citizens of the nation. Yet, as remarkable as the original text of the Constitution is, the first ten amendments to it—the Bill of Rights—are in some ways even more impressive and absolutely vital to Americans' ability to live freely in a democratic society.

Not all of the men who debated and drafted the Constitution initially believed that a Bill of Rights—guaranteeing states' rights and the particular rights reserved for individuals—was necessary or even desirable to include. Yet almost immediately after the Constitution was ratified, these men reconvened and began debating and drafting the first ten amendments to the United States' new governing document. Their labors produced one of the greatest protections of human freedom ever created. Taken together, the Bill of Rights has had more influence on the lives of ordinary citizens than almost any other amendments to the Constitution that followed it. A citizen enjoys rights guaranteed by it every time she watches television, goes to church, or attends a school board meeting.

Of particular concern to the authors of the Bill of Rights was the nation's criminal justice system. Their experience under the British during the pre-Revolutionary colonial era made it clear to them that in order to combat oppression and tyranny of the state, the criminal justice system must be as fair and as free from improper government interference as possible. An accused person must be given every possible guarantee of a fair trial. He or she must also be free from the fear of a government prosecuting him or her for political reasons. Also, the government must be restrained as much as possible, preventing it from violating the rights of an individual, because the law insists an individual is innocent until proven guilty.

The Fourth, Fifth, Sixth, and Eighth amendments to the U.S. Constitution all deal with what are known as the "rights of the accused." All offer not only specific protections for people accused of a crime but also impose restrictions on the kinds of actions that the government can take when it accuses someone of a crime. Among these amendments, the Fourth Amendment contains some of the most important and profound limitations on the powers of the government. Created in response to some of the worst abuses of justice that the British committed against the American colonists, the protections of the Fourth Amendment have long been considered a bedrock of American justice. However, it should be pointed out that, like all the protections of the Bill of Rights, it was not until the twentieth century that it finally came to protect all citizens of the United States equally, no matter what region of the country they lived in or what their race or gender.

In particular, the Fourth Amendment addresses searches and seizures and warrants. Legally, searches and seizures mean the ability of the government to search a person or her home or office and to seize items that provide evidence of a crime that the person may have committed. This evidence is gathered to use against her at trial. The Fourth Amendment requires that these searches and seizures be "reasonable." Interpreting and determining exactly what "reasonable" means has been the subject of many important Supreme Court decisions, and the working definition of "reasonable" changes with the times, but a reasonable search usually requires a warrant.

A warrant is a document, usually issued by a judge, that allows the police to search a person who is suspected of a crime or under arrest and any places associated with or belonging to that person, like a home, office, computer hard drive, or car. In order for the warrant to be issued, the government must demonstrate that it has probable cause to believe that the person covered in the warrant has committed a crime. In general, evidence that has been collected by a search performed without a warrant is not allowed to be used at trial. There are certain exceptions to this rule, however. The history of how this rule came to be part of the trial system, and exactly what the exceptions to it are, is another part of the interesting story of the Fourth Amendment.

As new technologies have been created, the "persons, houses, papers, and effects" that are protected by the Fourth Amendment have had to be redefined by the Supreme Court. Questions such as, "Can the police search a car without a warrant?" and "Is wiretapping illegal?" and "Can the police request transcripts of e-mails, texts, tweets, and cell phone voice mail from service providers?" have provoked some controversial decisions by the Court.

Along with the other protections guaranteed by the Bill of Rights, the Supreme Court has created an intricate, tightly controlled system dedicated to the principle that a person must be given every opportunity to prove his or her innocence and that the government must disprove that innocence beyond any reasonable doubt. This delicate balance between accused and accuser, citizen and government, has frequently become a source of controversy, as it has always been difficult to determine exactly how this balance should be maintained. But for two hundred years, the Bill of Rights and the U.S. Constitution have helped to guide those charged with the enormous duty of protecting the rights of American citizens.

But why do we have a Constitution or a Bill of Rights? Why are they necessary? Why can't we trust the government to rule fairly, respect its citizens' rights and freedoms, and not overstep its bounds? Why did the remarkable men behind the American Revolution feel the need to create a document that precisely laid out the functions of the national government? Why did they choose the form that the Constitution eventually took? And how has our interpretation of their vision changed over the two centuries since the Constitution was ratified? What does the Constitution and the Bill of Rights really mean in the end?

The answers to the first five questions can be found in the next few chapters. The rest of this book deals with the answers—if they exist—to the last two questions. But in a larger sense, there is no one way to say what the Constitution means. Its meaning is constantly changing, with the times, the nation's temper, and new technology, and as Americans continue to redefine exactly what its most important idea—liberty for all people—means to them today.

THE BRITISH AND COLONIAL ORIGINS OF FREEDOM FROM SEARCH AND SEIZURE

The American legal system owes much to the British. During the 150 years of British dominion over the American colonies, the laws, customs, and institutions of colonial government were either British or built along British models. For most of this time, in fact, this was a source of pride for the colonists, for they held that the British system was the finest in the world and that Britain guaranteed more freedom and justice than any other nation in Europe. Most of the Founding Fathers and the American colonists wished to avoid separation from and war with Britain. Instead, most of them merely wished to have their rights as Englishmen and British subjects acknowledged. It was a denial of these rights due to all British subjects—especially the right to have one's interests represented in Parliament—that led to the Declaration of Independence and revolution, not any inherent desire to found a new, more free and democratic society.

Like many other American governmental structures, philosophies, and founding documents, the Fourth Amendment to the Constitution both has its origins in British models and represents a conscious deviation from or reaction to those models. In this case, the Fourth Amendment owes its existence in large measure to a British custom of long standing: the general warrant.

General Warrants

A general warrant was a document that allowed government officials to arrest and search any person deemed suspicious and seize his or her possessions. While there were some restrictions on this practice in English common law, the government's search and seizure powers could be truly terrifying. A general warrant gave the government the unlimited right to break into a person's home or place of business and take his or her private papers and other personal, private, and intimate possessions, regardless of whether or not they had any bearing on the crime with which the person had been accused. Another kind of warrant, called a writ of assistance, made it possible for government officials to demand the assistance of other government officials or even bystanders in a search and seizure action.

The English had long prided themselves on their parliamentary institutions, the counterbalance they provided against the whims and potential tyranny of

Visitors to the Morgan Library and Museum in New York City gaze upon the earliest surviving manuscript copy of the Magna Carta on loan from the University of Oxford's Bodleian Library in England.

the monarchy, the representation they offered to ordinary English subjects, and the concept of limited and just government that had been enshrined in the Magna Carta of 1215. Yet despite the protections against tyrannical government provided for in the Magna Carta, governmental abuse of power was still not only a possibility but a reality. The general warrants were one particularly useful tool of such tyranny and abuse.

The general warrants were frequently used by the government to silence and punish those who disagreed with it. During the religious and civil upheavals of English society between 1500 and 1700, the warrants were used against Catholic dissenters and other opponents of the government. The officials responsible for executing the warrants were frequently accused of corruption, as it was believed that they kept items they had seized for their own personal use or enrichment, rather than turning them over as evidence in the case.

By the 1690s, however, political changes in England resulted in Parliament gaining much greater power than had previously been the case, increasing its leverage against the monarchy. The use of general warrants began to decline. Also, liberal-minded British legal theorists such as the famous Sir Edward Coke began to argue that the general warrant violated the Magna Carta and British common law. In fact, the Magna Carta has nothing to say about general warrants, but in time the argument came to be accepted by many.

The Document That Started It All: The Magna Carta

One of the most important documents in English history was the Magna Carta (Latin for "Great Charter"), issued by King John to his barons in 1215. This charter was important for several reasons. First, it was not simply granted by the king but was demanded by his subjects. Second, it made many reforms to the justice system in order to protect the rights of the English and to make the system more fair. Perhaps most important, it set out definite limits to the king's power and warned him that if he violated the charter, the barons had the right to rebel and try to remove him. Although the Magna Carta actually did little to help the common people of England (it was after all written by the nobility to protect themselves from the king), its principle—to limit the power of government and to guarantee certain rights—became the central idea of English law.

The Magna Carta, along with the English Bill of Rights of 1689, were not only the sources of the right to liberty the colonists felt was their due as Englishmen but also served as models for the U.S. Constitution and Bill of Rights.

Specific Warrants

Despite these changes in prevailing political philosophy and Parliament's growing authority and independence from the monarchy, general warrants continued to be used both in England and the American colonies.

However, in America, where many of the colonies had been founded upon principles of religious freedom, the general warrants were almost never used to persecute religious minorities, as had been the case in England.

Furthermore, in some of the northern colonies, experiments with a different kind of warrant, the specific warrant, had begun. Unlike a general warrant, a specific warrant named a particular place to be searched and the precise charges with which the person was being accused. More important, specific warrants limited what could be seized to only those items that were legitimate and relevant evidence of the crime the person was accused of committing.

Massachusetts was the first colony to use specific warrants. Although it later reverted to using general warrants, the principles behind the specific warrant remained part of the public consciousness and would be rekindled during the drafting of the Fourth Amendment. In the meantime, however, general warrants continued to be the order of the day in colonial America. Indeed, the use—and abuse—of general warrants can be viewed as being an indirect cause of anti-British sentiment in the colonies and a growing revolutionary fervor. This was particularly true in Massachusetts.

Writs of Assistance

In 1760, the death of King George II meant that the warrants he had issued would expire in six months, at which time new warrants would have to be obtained. One particular kind of warrant—a writ of assistance—was used by colonial customs officials to search colonists for smuggled goods. The warrant provided customs officials with the assistance of sheriffs, loyal subjects, and other officials in these search and seizure operations. Typically, these writs never expired. They were essentially permanent warrants, allowing customs officials to search colonists whenever and wherever they wanted, without having to apply for a new one each time a suspected smuggling operation sprang up. In addition, any place could be searched by the warrant holder, and he was not held responsible for any damage or loss caused by the search.

In anticipation of the rare expiration of all outstanding warrants following the death of King George II, a group of sixty-three Boston merchants, led and represented by attorney James Otis Jr., challenged the legality of these writs of assistance. They were opposed by a British customs agent named James Paxton. Otis argued that general warrants were illegal under the Magna Carta and common law, as well as the "higher law" and "natural law" of freedom and liberty. Otis eventually lost his case because his defense, while impassioned, contained many mistakes and misconceptions. Yet Otis's fiery arguments did much to increase the growing separation the colonists felt from the British. John Adams, one of the principal signers of the Declaration of Independence and later the second president of the United States, watched Paxton's case proceedings as a young man and later claimed that the American independence movement was born then and there.

James Otis Jr., pictured in this 1770 engraving, strongly opposed English colonial policy regarding both writs of assistance and the Stamp Act of 1765.

THE WILKES CASE

Shortly after Paxton's case, a series of proceedings known as Wilkes's case took place in England. John Wilkes had published a newspaper article that was

The image of John Wilkes, outspoken proponent of parliamentary liberty and a free press, appears on this 1770 enamel snuff box.

sharply critical of a speech made by King George III, in which the king endorsed the Paris Peace Treaty of 1763. This treaty ended the Seven Years' War between England, Prussia, and Portugal on one side and France, Spain, Austria, Russia, and Sweden on the other. Part of what inspired Wilkes's sharp-tongued wrath was the fact that King George's speech had been written by England's prime minister, John Stuart, 3rd Earl of Bute, Wilkes's political archenemy.

King George III was enraged by Wilkes's written attack, charged him with seditious libel (rebellion and slander), and issued general warrants for the arrest of Wilkes and the newspaper's publishers. Forty-nine people in all, including Wilkes, were arrested. Government officials searched their houses and seized thousands of books and personal papers. A defiant Wilkes proceeded to sue any and all of the officials connected to the search and seizure operations for unlawful trespass. He also challenged the constitutionality of general warrants and claimed parliamentary privilege (a kind of criminal immunity) for his article. At issue was whether the government could use a general warrant in an area where there was no law explicitly allowing them. Instead, there was merely the custom of issuing warrants in similar cases. The judge in the case, Charles Pratt, found that such warrants were indeed illegal under the Magna Carta. In a later case, he also found that personal papers could not be seized and used against a person, as that would force the person to incriminate himself.

General Warrants and the American Revolution

Wilkes's case was tried during the same time that the British Crown and Parliament were trying to take more direct control not only of the colonies' governments but their economies, too. General warrants had long been used in the colonies to enforce customs policies, particularly taxes on manufactured or imported goods. Now that the British government was increasing these taxes, it began to issue more general warrants to enforce them.

The colonists objected strenuously to both the increased taxes and the growing use of general warrants to enforce them. Only warrants issued by customary precedent, rather than through the mechanism of an explicit law allowing them, had been found to be unconstitutional in Wilkes's case. The warrants issued to enforce colonial tax policies, however, were based in law and therefore continued to be used without legal restriction. Growing resistance to the principle of the general warrant among colonists became almost the same thing as resistance to the British presence in the colonies and British rule over them. It is a telling fact that during the Revolution, when each state drafted its own constitution, eight of the twelve former colonies rejected the entire concept of general warrants and the search and seizure they made possible.

Following the Revolution, and even with independence won, however, some forms of general warrants continued to survive in the new nation. Because of this, and because of fears of the strong federal government created by the U.S. Constitution, there was a call for protection of citizens from this powerful tool of government in the Bill of Rights. James Madison's response was to draft an amendment that only allowed specific warrants, detailing exactly who and what was to be searched and for what reason. These warrants would have to be sought and obtained before each search; they did not offer permanent permission to search and seize randomly and at will.

In time, this brief addition to the Constitution would give Americans a greater freedom from searches and seizures than the citizens of any other country in the world have. The search and seizure provisions of the Bill of Rights are part of the larger story of the drafting and ratification of the Constitution and its first ten amendments and of the enshrinement of unprecedented rights and freedoms for American citizens.

FORMING A MORE PERFECT UNION

Even as the American Revolution raged and its outcome was far from certain, the colonies—now self-declared independent states—began to draft their own constitutions. In these documents, the states sought to guarantee their citizens the "natural" rights. These included freedom of speech and of the press, the right to trial by jury, and the freedom from the oppression of general warrants—the very rights they had been denied under colonial rule and that they were waging war to gain. All of these state constitutions called for governments composed of elected executives (governors) and legislatures, and many featured broad guarantees of individual citizens' rights. Some of these governing documents would become models for the later U.S. Constitution. What is most striking, however, is the need the colonists felt to create documents that would set forth precisely the powers, and limits on those powers, of government, providing a solid basis for determining the legality of any given law or act of government.

THE ARTICLES OF CONFEDERATION

In the immediate aftermath of the successful conclusion of the American Revolution, the new nation's chosen representatives did not initially create a national government along the same lines as those sketched by the various state constitutions. Instead, in the Articles of Confederation, they created a federal (or central) government with almost no power.

The Articles of Confederation provided for only a loose federation or union of the states. In fact, it did not term the collection of states a "nation" but rather a "league of friendship," bound by a sort of mutual defense pact. The Articles of Confederation granted the federal government limited authority to deal with questions of national importance, such as war and international diplomacy, but it generally left all other questions, including the idea of fundamental citizens' rights, up to the individual states.

There were several weaknesses with the arrangement. The Articles of Confederation provided for no executive branch, including no president, and there was no federal judiciary. The states retained most governing powers. The federal government was so weak that it couldn't even impose and collect taxes, regulate foreign and domestic commerce and trade, or draft and fund a standing army and navy. Each state could coin its own money and could place certain kinds of taxes, called duties and tariffs, on products imported from other American states. Because there was no executive branch charged with enforcing the laws, it was difficult to ensure that even the limited powers of

Congress would be respected. Also, any changes to the Articles of Confederation required the consent of all the states, not just a simple or even two-thirds majority, making it easy for one state to block necessary governmental reforms and improvements.

These defects in the new nation's governing document endangered the very existence of the United States in the first few years after the revolution. There was a very real danger that the already weak federal government might collapse altogether, leaving a loose collection of twelve small and relatively defenseless republics, with no international standing or alliances, clinging along the vulnerable eastern coast of North America. Because of this danger, a movement arose calling for a stronger and more stable central government that would address the faults of the Articles of Confederation and provide for a more purposeful and muscular—and truly united—league of states.

THE CONSTITUTIONAL CONVENTION

In 1787, after a strongly worded report supposedly written by New York's Alexander Hamilton, a leading critic of the Articles of Confederation, Congress issued a call for a Constitutional Convention that would meet to revise the Articles of Confederation. Once the states' designated representatives convened in

George Washington *(right)* consults with Thomas Jefferson *(seated, left)* and Alexander Hamilton *(standing)* in this 1790 painting by Constantino Brumidi. All three men played crucial roles in the 1787 Constitutional Convention.

Philadelphia, Pennsylvania, however, the convention quickly moved past this limited goal of revision. Instead, it began to draft an entirely new and re-imagined document that would not only replace the existing Articles of Confederation but fundamentally alter the political theories and principles underlying the government of the United States.

Each state except for Rhode Island sent a delegation of representatives to the Constitutional Convention. Many of the delegates were some of the ablest men of their generation. Thirty-nine of the fifty-five delegates had served in the Continental Congress before and during the revolution. Eight signers of the Declaration of Independence and more than thirty veterans of the Revolutionary War were in attendance. All of the delegates present were experienced in the government of their home states. The most influential participants in the convention were New York's Alexander Hamilton; Pennsylvania's James Wilson and Gouverneur Morris, who was eventually responsible for the Constitution's renowned preamble ("We the People..."); and Virginia's James Madison, the principal architect of the Constitution and, eventually, the Bill of Rights. George Washington even came out of retirement to serve as the Constitutional Convention's president.

Three major problems confronted the convention's delegates. First was the question of representation in the national government. There had to be a way to protect the small population states from being dominated by the large population states. At the same time, the large population states had to be given a say in the national government that corresponded in some way to the number of people they represented. A second challenge was creating an executive branch that would be able to adequately enforce national law without possessing so much power that it could become oppressive, overbearing, or corrupt. Finally, the third difficult question was how to resolve the many economic inadequacies of the original Articles of Confederation, including the federal government's right to tax the states, regulate interstate commerce and international trade, and be the exclusive printer of money (creating a federal currency, rather than each state printing and coining its own money). Each of these thorny problems prompted lengthy and passionate debate before a compromise suitable to all could be reached.

CONSTITUTIONAL PROBLEM SOLVING

The first problem confronting the Constitutional Convention was solved by the decision to have two separate houses of Congress. The lower house is the House of Representatives, where each state's representation would be proportional to its population (so each state's influence would be determined by its size). The upper house is the Senate, where each state would have two representatives (so each state's influence would be equal to the others, regardless of size). Each house was given different powers to help balance each other. The Senate, among other things, confirms Supreme Court justices and cabinet members, and ratifies treaties. The House, on the other hand, controls tax laws and breaks ties in presidential elections.

THE IMPORTANCE OF PRECEDENTS

One of the most important concepts in American justice is that of precedent, or as it is known in Latin, *stare decisis* (meaning "stand by what is decided"). In order for the U.S. justice system to work, a judge must follow the decisions of previous cases that are similar to the case he or she is currently judging.

For example, after the decision of the Supreme Court in *Miranda v. Arizona*—which requires that the police clearly inform a suspect of his constitutional rights when they arrest him—a judge in any case where a suspect was not read his rights would have to throw out any evidence that resulted from the arrest and possibly the entire case.

Precedents are important in maintaining a consistent series of laws and decisions about cases in the American justice system. The Supreme Court, however, is not bound to its own precedents. It may decide to ignore precedent and decide a case differently. This new decision then becomes precedent for the lower courts. The process is called reversal or overturning the previous decision. The Supreme Court does not reverse itself lightly or often. When it does, it usually justifies doing so for a number of reasons. For example, it may decide that the current case is different from the earlier decision. In such cases, the precedent may not change, as the ruling was strictly concerned with the current case. On the other hand, the Court may decide that the original ruling was a mistake and that the current ruling is correct. This may be because of changes to the nation since the original decision or faulty reasoning by the original Court. Whatever the Court does, however, its changes are the law of the land and binding on all lower courts.

The more common effect of Supreme Court decisions, however, is to modify earlier precedents by clarifying or restricting them with their new decision. In the middle of the twentieth century, the Supreme Court reversed many earlier decisions, resulting in a dramatic expansion of the rights of all U.S. citizens under the Constitution.

This kind of careful balancing and sharing of power is typical of the principle of "checks and balances" that would characterize the federal government under the Constitution. The new Constitution created three branches of federal government. The executive branch includes the president, the vice president, and the president's various cabinet offices and officers. The legislative branch is the law-making branch, composed of the House of Representatives and Senate. Finally, the judicial branch is composed of the U.S. Supreme Court and lower federal courts, which hear and decide cases that relate to the laws passed by Congress and the president. Each power given to one branch of government is balanced by the ability of another branch of government to review and overrule or correct that branch's decisions. In this way, no one branch of the federal government can acquire too much power and disregard and abuse the nation's

Both houses of the 110th Congress are sworn in at the U.S. Capitol in Washington, D.C.

laws, the Constitution, or its protections of individual rights and freedoms.

Some of the best examples of checks and balances can be seen in how the convention solved the second of their major problems, the creation of an executive branch. They needed to give the president enough power so he or she could enforce the nation's laws but not so much that he or she could become a tyrant. The answer was to split powers between the president and Congress. For example, the president is the commander in chief of all U.S. armed forces, but only Congress can declare war or provide funds for the military. The president can veto a law Congress passes, but Congress can override the president's veto if two-thirds of its members vote in favor of doing so. In this way, most of the delegates to the Constitutional Convention were satisfied that they had created an executive branch that could not become tyrannical.

The last of the three problems was perhaps the easiest to resolve. Congress was given the ability to tax the entire nation. States were forbidden to coin their own money, and Congress was given the power to regulate commerce between them.

In addition to the legislative branch (Congress) and executive branch (the president) of government, the Constitution provided for the powers of a judicial branch—the Supreme Court and lower federal courts. The powers given to the Supreme Court were initially

President Barack Obama salutes a military honor guard. One of the president's powers granted by the Constitution is to serve as commander in chief of the armed forces.

somewhat limited. Its work was mostly confined to deciding disputes between the states, between the federal government and state governments, and between the federal government and foreign governments. Soon after ratification of the Constitution, however, the Supreme Court would come into its own by asserting perhaps its most important power: deciding whether or not a state or federal law was constitutional.

FEDERALISTS VS. ANTI-FEDERALISTS

The Constitution in its original form had remarkably little to say about the rights of citizens of the United States. It did forbid the granting of noble titles and the passing of laws that make something a crime only after the act has been committed (known as ex post facto laws). The Constitution also forbade laws that pass judgment on a person without a trial, known as bills of attainder. Although some of the delegates to the Constitutional Convention argued for inclusion of a statement detailing and guaranteeing the basic rights of citizens, the majority felt that the checks and balances already placed upon the federal government adequately protected the rights of people.

While the Constitution was in many ways superior to the Articles of Confederation, it still provoked a firestorm of criticism during the debate on its ratification. Some charged that the convention had acted illegally in deciding to radically change the structure of government, rather than just modifying the existing Articles of Confederation. Many also felt that the states lost too much power under the Constitution. Still others feared that the new government, and especially the president, would be too powerful and oppress the people. It had, after all, been only eleven years since the start of the Revolution, and many people remained suspicious of any central authority.

The two sides in this passionate debate over the proposed new Constitution became known as the Federalists, who were in favor of the Constitution and a strong central government, and the Anti-Federalists, who opposed the Constitution and favored states' rights and decentralized authority. Alexander Hamilton, James Madison, and John Jay were leaders of the Federalist cause. Their essays, collected as the Federalist Papers, are brilliant arguments in favor of the Constitution and did much to swing public opinion to the side of the Federalists.

THE UNITED STATES: A FEDERAL REPUBLIC

The American system of government is sometimes called a federal republic, and the national government is generally referred to as the federal government. But what do these words mean? What makes the United States a federal republic?

Essentially, federalism refers to a division of powers. Local governments agree to give up some of their powers to a larger government that can act on their behalf. In the United States, the basic units of federalism are the states and the national government.

The Constitution makes clear this basic division. The federal government is given certain powers—the right to coin money, the right to declare war, the right to regulate commerce between the states—that each state is forbidden to do. On the other hand, the Constitution gave only very specific powers to the federal government. All other matters were to be left to the states. This was reinforced by passage of the Bill of Rights. The Tenth Amendment further supports this idea by noting that those powers not specifically given to the federal government, or denied to the states, are reserved for the states, or "the people."

The debate over ratification was most intense in the large population states of Virginia, Massachusetts, and New York. Massachusetts narrowly ratified the Constitution only after it recommended a number of Anti-Federalist–supported amendments be made to it. In Virginia, James Madison led the Federalist cause to a narrow victory, but only by promising to consider a Bill of Rights that would be added to the Constitution. With Virginia and Massachusetts in line, New York soon followed. Although it would take more than two years for the last two states— North Carolina and Rhode Island—to ratify the Constitution, the decision of the three largest and most important states to support the governing document made its eventual ratification inevitable. In 1789, the Constitution became the law of the land.

AMENDING THE CONSTITUTION:
THE BILL OF RIGHTS

Following the ratification of the Constitution and the creation of Congress, James Madison, despite sometimes intense opposition in Virginia, managed to be elected to the House of Representatives. Once there, as promised, he began work on a series of amendments to the Constitution that would become the Bill of Rights. He fulfilled this promise to his fellow Virginians even though at the Constitutional Convention he had argued that such a bill was unnecessary. Yet despite his earlier opposition, Madison turned to the task with great skill and efficiency, creating a legacy of liberty still enjoyed by U.S. citizens today.

Madison originally proposed, and persuaded the House of Representatives to approve, seventeen amendments to the Constitution. The Senate failed to approve the last five of these. Of the twelve amendments that were sent to the states for approval, only the last ten achieved ratification right away. Originally, Madison wanted the amendments to be inserted directly into the Constitution, but it was decided instead to place them at the end of the document.

ENUMERATED AND UNENUMERATED RIGHTS

James Madison, pictured in this 1800 portrait, was the driving force behind the drafting and ratification of the Bill of Rights.

While it may seem completely sensible to us today that the Constitution should make a basic statement listing and guaranteeing the rights of its citizens, the Federalists had several arguments as to why they had not done so in the original document. One reason was that they felt that it was the states, not the federal government, that would be the principal guardians of the people's freedom. This was an especially useful argument to make against those who felt that the states were losing too much power to the central government.

Others feared that if specific rights were mentioned in the Constitution, the government might oppress the people by recognizing only those rights and no others. In other words, by enumerating, or listing, only a few rights, the government might in effect take away all other rights, even those long deemed the "natural"

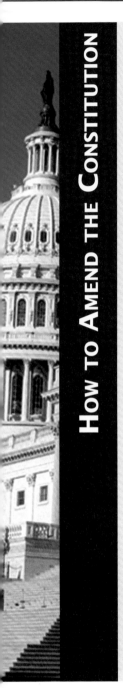

HOW TO AMEND THE CONSTITUTION

Article V of the U.S. Constitution lays out the procedures for amending, or changing, the U.S. Constitution. There are two ways that this can be accomplished. The first way is for two-thirds of each house of Congress to approve an amendment and send it to the state legislatures to be ratified. The second way, which has never actually happened, is for two-thirds of the state legislatures to call for a convention to write new amendments; this would be almost the same as calling a new constitutional convention.

In either case, the new amendment must be approved by three-fourths of the state legislatures. Once that has happened, the amendment is a part of the Constitution and only another amendment may change it.

Amendments have a history all their own in constitutional studies. The original Constitution forbade any amendments that threatened slavery prior to 1808. Only one amendment has specifically repealed another amendment, although many amendments have had effects on other amendments. The Twenty-First Amendment, for example, repealed the Eighteenth Amendment, which had made alcoholic beverages illegal in the United States. However, the most important example in this book is the effect of the Fourteenth Amendment on the original ten amendments of the Bill of Rights.

Thirty-three amendments have been proposed and twenty-seven ratified. The last, curiously enough, was one of the oldest amendments proposed.

rights of free men and women. These fears led to the inclusion of the Ninth and Tenth amendments to the Constitution.

The Ninth Amendment states that even if a right is not enumerated, or explicitly mentioned, in the Constitution, it should not be understood to be a right denied to citizens. In other words, the American people are entitled to a host of personal freedoms and individual rights that are not mentioned in the body of the Constitution. It is the job of the courts to decide what these rights are. The Tenth Amendment states that any right not granted specifically to the federal government and not explicitly denied to the states in the Constitution shall be reserved for the states or the people.

Protecting a Proper Functioning Democracy

The other eight amendments that constitute the Bill of Rights similarly reflect Madison's growing conviction that the original Constitution required additional protections and guarantees of certain rights in order to create a properly functioning democracy. The Bill of Rights, of which Madison was the chief architect, reflects this belief in the fundamental civil rights possessed by each and every American citizen.

The First Amendment, for example, guarantees the right to freedom of speech, the press, assembly, and religion—all the vital needs of a varied and democratic population. The Second and Third amendments recall the colonists' struggle against the British, preserving the right to bear arms and freedom from the quartering of troops among civilians in peacetime. The Fifth Amendment provides a guarantee against self-incrimination; the necessity for the government to get an indictment by a grand jury (meaning that a jury of citizens must decide that enough evidence exists to charge a person with a crime) before trying a person; the right to be tried only once for a crime (the "double-jeopardy" clause); and the guarantee that the government will give an accused person a full and fair trial (the "due process" clause). The Fifth Amendment also guarantees that the government will not take land or property from a person for its use without compensating him or her for it.

The Sixth Amendment guarantees a speedy trial and an impartial jury composed of people from the region in which the crime was committed. It also ensures the accused person the right to confront the people accusing him and as well as any witnesses to the crime. The Sixth Amendment further guarantees that the accused has the ability to bring witnesses for his or her defense and the right to a lawyer or counsel to assist in the defense. The Seventh

Protesters opposed to government policies rally in front of the U.S. Capitol in an effort to remind legislators of the importance and meaning of the Constitution and the rights and freedoms it guarantees.

Amendment guarantees the right to a trial by jury in civil cases where the amount in damages or other compensation sought is greater than $20. The Eighth Amendment prohibits cruel and unusual punishment at the hands of law enforcement and within the criminal justice system.

LEGISLATING POST-COLONIAL ANXIETIES

It is important to note that the intent of the Bill of Rights was primarily to protect the majority from the minority—the large number of ordinary, powerless American citizens from the relatively small number of powerful Congressional representatives, judges, government officials, and other political or business elites. The lingering fear of the generation that suffered under tyrannical colonial rule, fought the revolution, and wrote the Constitution was not so much that an individual or small minority might be deprived of their individual rights but that a tyrannical central government would rob the American people as a whole of their rights. This had been the colonists' experience of British rule before the revolution, and it was not something they ever wanted to see repeated.

The Anti-Federalists' demands for a Bill of Rights had been founded upon this fear of a tyrannical central government, and the wording of the Bill of Right's ten amendments seeks to calm their fears. The language of the Bill of Rights, with its heavy use of negatives, is much more concerned with prohibiting the federal government from interfering with the rights of the people than in asserting what those rights actually were. They are as much an enumeration of what powers the federal government does not possess as they are a listing of the rights that American citizens do possess.

The Bill of Rights is also unusual in that most of the amendments do not strip the federal government of powers it once had or grant it new powers. Rather, they speak specifically to what the government is simply not permitted to do. They are an expression of governmental limitation—of the limits and boundaries of federal power. In effect, the Bill of Rights seeks to shield the people from the potentially tyrannical power of their own government. Nowhere are these limits upon government power—and potential abuse of power—more apparent than in the Fourth Amendment and its protections against "unreasonable" and unlawful search and seizure.

THE FOURTH AMENDMENT AND SEARCH WARRANTS

The Fourth Amendment protects people from "unreasonable" searches of their persons, houses, papers, and effects (personal possessions). But what constitutes an unreasonable search? What guidelines exist constitutionally to help determine whether or not a search is prohibited by the Fourth Amendment?

The text of the amendment itself offers no definition of either a "reasonable" or an "unreasonable" search. Some have argued that this meant that the interpretation of the amendment had to be guided by both common law (what has traditionally been viewed as reasonable or unreasonable, based in part on prior legal precedent) and the opinion of the judge hearing the case to decide whether or not a search was unreasonable. Others have argued that the amendment merely provides a person who has been the victim of an unreasonable search the ability to sue the people responsible for the search, including those who planned, ordered, and carried it out.

However, for the most part, judges at all levels of the judiciary system—from local and state judges to federal circuit and appeals court judges, and all the way up to Supreme Court justices—have relied on the second part of the Fourth Amendment for guidance. This part of the amendment requires that warrants be issued only with "probable cause" and that they be specific, limited warrants that name the person or place to be searched. Using this clause as a guide, a search can be considered reasonable only if a proper warrant has been issued. However, the Court has recognized that there are circumstances when the public good requires that a search be performed without a warrant. Determining the precise circumstances in which a warrantless search can be "reasonable" has always spurred great controversy.

EXCEPTIONS TO WARRANT REQUIREMENTS

One important factor to note is that searches conducted by a private citizen are not covered by the Fourth Amendment. It is only when the government and government-sanctioned law enforcement step in to search a person that his or her constitutional protections are triggered. In the 1921 case of *Burdeau v. McDowell*, the Court ruled that the Fourth Amendment did not protect J. C. McDowell, who, after being fired by his employers, had had his office safe opened up by company officials and the contents of it and his desk handed over to the federal Justice Department. This

Officers from the Los Angeles Police Department's Gang Unit search an apartment for stolen police ammunition.

evidence was used to convict McDowell of mail fraud. He appealed to the Supreme Court to overturn the conviction based on his Fourth Amendment rights. The Court refused to do so, noting that he could still sue his former employers for damages.

One exception to the warrant requirement is the "plain view" exception. Basically, this allows police who are lawfully in an area to seize evidence not specifically covered by a warrant. For example, if a policeman were to witness two people taking illegal drugs in public, he would not need a warrant to arrest them and seize the drugs. Likewise, if during a search of a house (with a proper search warrant) for the murder weapon used in a recent robbery, a policewoman sees the stolen goods from that robbery lying around, she could seize them and they could later be used as evidence of guilt in a criminal trial, even though these items were not specifically included in the original search warrant. However, the stolen items must be in plain view, not hidden inside a drawer or locked in a closet.

REQUIREMENTS FOR OBTAINING A SEARCH WARRANT

There are two basic factors necessary to obtain a warrant to search or arrest someone: probable cause and a neutral magistrate. Both are required in order to generate a search warrant that does not violate the Fourth Amendment.

Probable cause means that there is enough evidence to convince a magistrate—an official such as a judge charged with administering the laws—that a crime has been committed by the person whom the warrant is to be issued against. In cases of search warrants, both the place to be searched and the crime that has been committed must be specifically stated. It is possible that any evidence of the crime that is gathered will not be admissible in court if it was not mentioned in the search warrant or was found outside of the area specified in the warrant.

APPEALING TO THE SUPREME COURT

The Supreme Court actually has a very restricted direct jurisdiction, mainly limited to resolving issues between the states, or between the United States and foreign powers. What makes the Court so powerful in interpreting the nation's laws, however, is its power to review appeals.

The Supreme Court sits on top of the nation's federal court system and is that system's ultimate court of appeal. It can also hear appeals from the highest court that hears appeals in each state.

In order to hear an appeal, a federal court—including the Supreme Court—must decide that there is a "federal question" involved in the case. A federal question is one that relates to an act of Congress, a treaty, or a constitutional question. Since the adoption of the Fourteenth Amendment, many cases have been heard in federal court in an attempt to answer the following question: to what degree does a right contained in the Bill of Rights also apply to the states?

Most cases come to the Supreme Court by means of a writ of certiorari. This petition, which was authorized by Congress is 1925, is a petition that the losing side can file with the Court asking it to review a lower court's decision. If four justices vote to hear the case, certiorari is granted and the Court will decide the matter.

Each side will then prepare papers, called briefs, that detail not only the reasons why they think the original decision should be overturned or upheld but also the past cases that they think provide precedents for how the present case should be decided. Each side also gets the chance to speak before the Court. At the end of the process, the justices consider each side's argument

and then take a vote. The decision of the majority becomes the final decision on the case. The majority must, and the minority may, then prepare a statement, called an opinion, explaining the reasons they voted the way they did.

Evidence used for probable cause does not have to meet the tougher standards of evidence used at trial. However, it must be made under "oath or affirmation" according to the Fourth Amendment, and it must be supported by facts. In other words, the government cannot get a warrant just because it suspects a person has committed a crime. Rather, law enforcement must have other evidence that supports the idea that not only was a crime committed but also that the person they are investigating could have committed it. On the other hand, hearsay evidence— testimony by people who did not actually observe the event they are describing but merely heard about it from a third person—can be used to obtain a search warrant, even though such evidence cannot be used at trial. However, in the 1978 case of *Franks v. Delaware*, a warrant obtained by lying to the judge or magistrate was ruled to be unconstitutional, and the evidence gathered as a result was deemed inadmissible in court.

Warrants are only necessary if a person does not consent to a search. That is, the police may always ask a person if they can search him or her or his or her space (such as a home, office, or car). It is only when that person refuses to allow them to do so that they must get a warrant. However, in the 1973 case of *Schneckloth v. Bustamonte*, the Court ruled that the police, although they must ask to conduct a search, do not have to inform the person that he or she has the right to refuse to allow them to search. In 1974, the Court further found that one occupant of a house may consent to a search of the building, even if the other occupant is not there to give his or her consent. Any evidence found against the person who was not present to give his or her consent or refusal would be admissible in court.

NEUTRAL MAGISTRATES

Crucial to the warrant process is the concept of the neutral magistrate. In other words, the party that grants the warrant must not have an interest in the case. This is why police departments cannot issue their own search warrants. They have an interest in gathering evidence against certain suspects, so they cannot be expected to make an impartial decision about whether probable cause exists. In many cases, they have already decided probable cause does exist, which is why they want to conduct a search of a suspect in the first place. This is where judges come in.

A lawyer and a judge confer at the bench. Law enforcement officials must convince judges, with sworn affidavits, that there is probable cause to issue a search warrant. The warrant must specifically state what is being searched for and exactly where the search will be conducted.

Judges are charged with being impartial. They are not part of the police or prosecutor's department. Therefore they can, in theory at least, be trusted to judge fairly whether probable cause exists for the issuing of a search warrant. This was emphasized by the Court's decision in the 1971 case of *Coolidge v. New Hampshire*, where a warrant had been issued by a state official who was also the chief prosecutor of the case. The Court threw out all the evidence gathered under this warrant.

THE WARREN COURT AND THE RIGHTS OF THE ACCUSED

Earl Warren (1891–1974) was one of the most active and influential chief justices in Supreme Court history. Under his tenure, the protections of the Bill of Rights were expanded to include all people living in the United States.

Before becoming the chief justice of the Supreme Court, Warren had spent over thirty years in public office, most famously as governor of California (1943–1953). In 1953, he was appointed to be chief justice of the Supreme Court by President Dwight D. Eisenhower. When Warren's rulings as chief justice turned out to be much more liberal than the conservative Eisenhower had wanted, he called the appointment "the worst mistake of my life." Others would dispute that, however.

Warren made many rulings that affected race relations in the United States. One of the most famous of these was the decision in *Brown v. Board of Education* (1954), which overturned the "separate but equal" doctrine that had prevailed for over sixty years, ordering the desegregation of public schools.

Warren's Court also made many rulings that profoundly changed the rights of the accused in the United States. In *Miranda v. Arizona* (1966), the Court found that police could not question a person unless he or she was made to understand all of his or her constitutionally protected rights. This is the source of the famous "Miranda rights" that the police must read to any person they arrest ("You have the right to remain silent," etc.). In 1963, *Gideon v. Wainwright* found that in order for trials to be fair, the courts must appoint lawyers to anyone who cannot afford one. And in 1961, the decision in *Mapp v. Ohio* expanded Fourth Amendment protections to everyone in the United States.

Warren's tenure was filled with controversy. The decisions of the Court during this time were often criticized by conservatives as being too "soft on crime." (Another controversial event during his tenure as chief justice was service as chairman of the commission that investigated the assassination of President John F. Kennedy.) When he retired in 1969, President Richard M. Nixon moved to appoint a more conservative chief justice in the hope of restricting or reversing some of the decisions of the Warren Court.

Earl Warren died in 1974. His legacy of expanding the protections of the Bill of Rights, however, remains substantially unchanged.

On the other hand, there is no constitutional requirement that the magistrate issuing a search warrant be a judge or even a lawyer. The 1972 case of *Shadwick v. City of Tampa, Fla.*, found that a municipal court clerk could issue a warrant for municipal offenses. However, the magistrate in question must normally be involved in deciding cases involving crimes described in the warrant. Therefore, for serious criminal offenses, judges are usually required to obtain a search warrant.

IMPORTANT FOURTH AMENDMENT PRECEDENTS

The Fourth Amendment protects people from unreasonable searches and seizures. It does this primarily by requiring the government and its agents to obtain a warrant before they can even begin to make a search. However, how can the Fourth Amendment protect a person if a warrant is wrongly issued or if the police overstep the restrictions of the warrant? What recourse does a person who is being tried under those conditions have under the Fourth Amendment? The answer to these questions involves some of the most controversial decisions made by the Supreme Court. The evolution of the extent and range of Fourth Amendment protections took many years and involved several complex Supreme Court decisions.

The most urgent and compelling question that the Court was forced to address was this: How can the rules of evidence, the guidelines for whether or not a piece of evidence can be used in a trial, be constructed in order to conform to the Fourth Amendment? And what can be done to guarantee fairness in trials and for the accused when the government violates the Fourth Amendment, even without meaning to?

BOYD V. UNITED STATES

The first major Fourth Amendment decision was the 1886 case of *Boyd v. United States*. This case involved a supplier of plate glass, E. A. Boyd, who had been contracted to make glass for several federal buildings in Philadelphia, Pennsylvania. In return for discounting their price, the Boyds had asked the federal government to be allowed to import the glass without paying a special tax, called a duty, which was normally required.

However, the government soon had cause to suspect that the Boyds were actually cheating the system, by importing more glass than they needed for the job, as a way of getting around the duty and obtaining large quantities of duty-free glass for use on other jobs. The federal government took the Boyds to court, demanding that the contract be forfeited. During the trial, the judge ordered the Boyds to produce all their invoices for the glass that had been imported. The Boyds protested but eventually gave in and were convicted based upon this paper trail of evidence. They then appealed the decision, claiming that their Fourth Amendment right of freedom from unreasonable seizures and Fifth

U.S. Marshals descend upon the offices of the Stanford Financial Group in Houston, Texas. The financial services company was being investigated for, and ultimately charged with, fraud.

Amendment right against self-incrimination had been violated.

In considering the case, the Supreme Court had to examine carefully both constitutional amendments and decide what should be done if they had in fact been violated. In the end, the Supreme Court sided with the Boyds. By ordering them to produce the paperwork, the lower court judge had indeed violated both the Fourth and Fifth Amendment rights of the defendants. In fact, the two amendments were found to have much in common with each other, for clearly the right to be "secure" in one's person or dwelling means that a person should not be forced to give up evidence that might be incriminating. The Court ordered not only that the Boyds conviction be reversed but also that a new trial take place, one in which the incriminating evidence could not be used.

WEEKS V. UNITED STATES AND THE EXCLUSIONARY RULE

Another major landmark in Fourth Amendment judicial history came out of the 1914 case of *Weeks v. United States*, when, for the first time, the Court laid down guidelines for the kinds of searches that could be permitted under the amendment. This and a series of further decisions soon established two rules of evidence. The first of these, the exclusionary rule, is still used today, while the second, the "mere evidence" rule, was abandoned in the 1970s.

In the Boyd case, the Court had ordered a new trial to remedy a conviction based upon improperly acquired evidence. However, this solution was impractical on a large scale. If every trial conviction that hinged upon disputed evidence were overturned and retried, the expenses would be enormous, as would the growing backlog of cases. The justice system would grind to a halt. To remedy this problem, the Court created the exclusionary rule in *Weeks v. United States* (1914).

The case involved the arrest of Fremont Weeks and the search of his home, all without a warrant. Weeks was suspected of using the U.S. mail system to run an illegal lottery. On the basis of evidence resulting from these warrantless searches, he was convicted at trial. Weeks appealed his case to the Supreme Court, claiming his Fourth Amendment rights had been violated.

The Supreme Court agreed with Weeks, not only overturning his conviction but also adopting a controversial new policy in the process: evidence that had been seized in violation of the Fourth Amendment could not be used at trial. This meant that during a trial, a defendant could move that evidence being used by the government be "excluded" if the defense felt that it had been acquired illegally. This judicial precedent would have profound effects on the American justice system and the rights of defendants.

RAMIFICATIONS OF THE *WEEKS* DECISION

Just as the decision in *Boyd v. United States* had noted the close relationship between the Fourth and Fifth amendments, the Supreme Court's *Weeks* decision had ramifications for evidence issues covered by other amendments as well. In the years ahead, the Supreme Court would conclude that any evidence gathered that would violate the Fifth Amendment protection against self-incrimination had to be excluded. In 1920, the Court ruled that all evidence illegally seized was inadmissible, even photocopies. However, some evidence that cannot be used to establish that a person has committed a crime can still be used to impeach his or her credibility, for example, by establishing that a person has lied during testimony and under oath (which is itself a crime known as perjury).

At this point in U.S. judicial history, the rules of evidence the Court had created, including the exclusionary rule, still applied only to the federal government. Any search and seizures conducted by state officials fell under state law and were seen as beyond the jurisdiction of the Fourth Amendment. This was affirmed again in the 1949 case of *Wolf v. Colorado*, centering upon the illegal abortions provided by Julius A. Wolf.

The case involved only actions taken on a state level. Evidence used in the case, however, would have been excluded in a federal court due to its being illegally obtained. Despite the improperly obtained evidence, the Supreme Court did not overturn the state court's conviction. The justices' decision did,

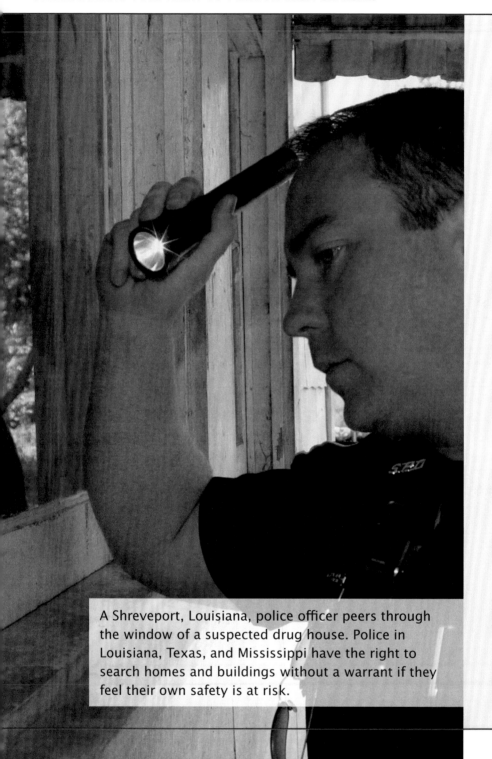

A Shreveport, Louisiana, police officer peers through the window of a suspected drug house. Police in Louisiana, Texas, and Mississippi have the right to search homes and buildings without a warrant if they feel their own safety is at risk.

however, find that the Fourteenth Amendment extended the Fourth Amendment protections at the state level but that the states were not required to obey the exclusionary rule, provided that they had other means of preventing illegal searches. In fact, at the time, only seventeen states had exclusionary rules similar to those the Supreme Court created in the *Weeks* decision. Indeed, only if a state had enacted laws allowing for searches and seizures in violation of exclusionary rule guidelines would the Fourteenth Amendment allow the case to be overturned by a federal court. This apparent contradiction was not firmly resolved until the *Mapp v. Ohio* decision (see next section).

Another problem that *Weeks* created was the so-called "silver platter" doctrine. Basically, this allowed federal prosecutors to use evidence that would normally be inadmissible—because the searches or seizures were in violation of the federal rules of evidence—provided that it had been uncovered by state agents, acting without federal help. Because the states were not bound by the Fourth Amendment, they could conduct illegal searches and then hand the evidence to the federal prosecutors on a "silver platter." This situation managed to exist even after the *Wolf* case found that the Fourth Amendment did indeed apply, in principle, to the states. The "silver platter" doctrine was not overturned until 1960.

STATES AND THE EXCLUSIONARY RULE: *MAPP V. OHIO*

Prior to 1961, all cases relating to Fourth Amendment challenges were federal ones, decided by federal courts, and pertaining only to actions taken by federal government officials. It was not until the landmark decision in *Mapp v. Ohio* (1961) that the Fourth Amendment was found to apply to the states as well as the federal government. The decision in *Mapp v. Ohio* finally resolved the confusing gray area existing between state and federal evidence gathering practices and federal judicial jurisdiction over them, but in doing so it created even more controversy.

In 1957, the police came to Dollree Mapp's house in Cleveland, demanding to search it for a person who was wanted for questioning in connection with a recent bombing. Rather than let them in right away, Mapp called an attorney and then refused to let the police come in until they produced a search warrant. The police then left.

When they came back, they forced their way inside, waving in her face a piece of paper they claimed to be a warrant. She snatched it away and stuffed it in her bosom, but the police forcibly retrieved it. They then searched the house and found books, pictures, and photographs that were

Dollree Mapp *(center)* was arrested in Queens, New York, in 1957, following a warrantless search of her apartment. The evidence collected during this illegal search was eventually thrown out following a landmark Supreme Court decision in her favor.

considered obscene under Ohio law. Dollree Mapp was arrested, tried, and convicted for possession of such materials.

Mapp's appeal eventually reached the Supreme Court, which ruled to overturn her conviction. In doing so, the justices also applied the exclusionary rule to the states. Justice Tom Clark noted, in the majority opinion, "Nothing can destroy a government more quickly than its failure to observe its own laws, or worse, its disregard to the charter of its own existence…"

Since its inception, the exclusionary rule had been controversial. Often, removing one piece of evidence from the prosecution's case can completely wreck any chance of convicting a person of a crime, even if he or she is guilty. The chance that a criminal can go free because of a "technicality" is increased by the exclusionary rule. As Benjamin Cardozo, a famous New York judge, put it before he served as a Supreme Court justice, "The criminal is to go free because the constable has blundered."

Others, however, have said that not only does the exclusionary rule protect the highest principles of American liberty, but that sometimes the guilty must be allowed to go free in order for the innocent not to be convicted. The results of corrupt, sloppy, or oppressive search and seizures should not be admissible in court because law enforcement will then operate on the assumption that evidence rules don't really have to be followed. They will feel free to abuse their authority, which means that anyone—even the innocent—can become the victim of an illegal, inappropriate, or abusive search and have their Fourth Amendment rights violated.

THE BURGER COURT

Curiously enough, the man who was hand-picked to limit the liberal reforms of Earl Warren was named Warren Earl Burger. Born in 1907 in St. Paul, Minnesota, Warren Burger had a long career as a conservative judge before being chosen by President Nixon to be the replacement for the retiring Earl Warren as chief justice of the U.S. Supreme Court.

However, Burger did not overrule any of the key decisions of the Warren Court. He helped to reaffirm the famous *Miranda* decision, despite the harsh criticism of that ruling by both the president and many law-enforcement personnel throughout the country. Although his Court did indeed limit some of the decisions of the Warren Court, Burger's term was not marked by a firm stand on any particular ideology, but rather with pragmatic concerns of justice and applicability.

In 1973, the Burger Court issued a controversial decision of their own: *Roe v. Wade*, which made abortion legal throughout America. Perhaps just as controversial as the abortion aspects of the case was the assertion that there existed a "right to privacy" that was implied within the Bill of Rights, even though no such protection was spelled out. This example of "loose constructionalism," or interpreting the Constitution beyond what the Founders clearly laid out, was criticized by many who felt that the Constitution should be interpreted more conservatively.

After Burger's retirement in 1986, he served as chairman of the committee that planned the celebration of the Constitution's two-hundredth anniversary in 1988. He died in 1995.

Still, the decision in *Mapp* was highly controversial, for it forced all of the states to follow the exclusionary rule from that moment forward. This ruling, along with several other Supreme Court decisions of this era, under Chief Justice Earl Warren, expanded the federal rights of the accused found in the Bill of Rights to the states. This led many to feel that the Court was protecting criminals at the expense of law-abiding citizens. Thus, the more conservative Supreme Court of the 1970s and 1980s refused to continue to expand the exclusionary rule and, in many places, found exceptions to it. For example, the Court did not expand the exclusionary rule to include grand juries, special juries that decide whether or not to issue an indictment. An indictment is a formal statement accusing a person of committing a crime.

FURTHER EXCEPTIONS TO THE EXCLUSIONARY RULE

In 1984, two important exceptions to the exclusionary rule were permitted by the Court. The case of *United States v. Leon* addressed an invalid filing of a California search warrant. The police had requested a warrant to search the houses and cars of several people accused of various drug crimes. In the affidavit filed in order to receive a search warrant, they included factual errors to disguise their lack of probable cause. The warrant was

Officers from the Los Angeles Police Department's Gang Unit
search several men caught drinking alcoholic beverages
in public.

approved and issued by a magistrate. On the basis of
evidence seized under this warrant, the people were
convicted. However, the evidence used to obtain the
warrant was not technically admissible under California
procedures because it was later deemed that the police
did not have probable cause to request the warrant.
The question for the Court was whether or not such a
technical mistake should invalidate the search.

They ruled that it did not. Though the police had
acted in bad faith by misrepresenting the evidence
providing probable cause for a search, the magistrate

had acted in good faith when approving the warrant because he was not aware of the deception. The magistrate had simply made his decision based on the information put before him. Under these circumstances, the search could be considered legal.

The other important exception granted that year was "inevitable discovery." This means that if the prosecution can demonstrate that other evidence ultimately would have led the police to evidence that had been illegally seized, the otherwise impermissible evidence would then be admissible at trial.

The "good faith" exception of *Leon* continued to be expanded during the 1980s and 1990s. In 1987, the Court ruled that a search and seizure conducted under a law that was later declared unconstitutional was another example of the "good faith" provision. A similar case decided that even if the police went to the wrong apartment, a search or seizure might be considered legal if they were acting in "good faith."

And in 1995, the case of *Arizona v. Evans* extended the provision to include errors by the magistrate, not the police. A search was conducted by the police under a warrant, which, although it appeared to be valid, had actually been "quashed," or suppressed. However, a computer error meant that the police were not notified in time. The Court ruled that the search was legal. Clerical errors made by the court's employees did not provide grounds for the exclusionary rule.

Gouled v. United States: The "Mere Evidence" Rule

In the 1921 case of *Gouled v. United States*, the Court was asked to decide exactly what kind of evidence could be searched for under the Fourth Amendment. A friend of Felix Gouled had come to his place of business at the request of federal agents and removed several papers. These papers were later used to convict Gouled of defrauding the government in the fulfillment of certain defense contracts.

Gouled appealed to the Supreme Court, claiming his Fourth and Fifth Amendment rights had been violated. The Court upheld this part of his defense, as the *Weeks* decision clearly seemed to apply here, since the search had been warrantless and performed under false pretenses. However, it further ruled that the type of evidence used against Gouled was inadmissible as well. The documents did not relate to the crime but merely provided evidence that it had been committed. The Court ruled that only those items that were either the "fruits or instrumentalities" of a crime could be admitted as evidence. For example, a painting stolen in a robbery could be used as evidence, as it was the "fruit" of a crime. A gun used to commit murder could be evidence, since it was an "instrumentality" of the crime. But, as the *Gouled* decision showed, letters that merely indicated a person had committed a crime could not be used as evidence against a person.

The Court's decision was based on the theory that the Fourth Amendment also protected the property of a person. Property interests were an important subject for the Court in the nineteenth and early twentieth centuries, and the Court tended to be very conservative in matters concerning private property, usually siding with the citizen against the government and law enforcement. In the *Gouled* case, the Supreme Court had decided that the property and privacy interests of an individual were greater than the public interest of the government.

While the *Gouled* decision would seem to severely restrict warrants, in actual practice it did not have a great effect. Federal law never allowed warrants for "mere evidence." However, the states could still issue warrants designed to gather a broad variety of evidence, many only loosely connected to a crime.

OVERTURNING THE MERE EVIDENCE RULE: *WARDEN V. HAYDEN*

The mere evidence rule also suffered from difficulties of interpretation. What might be mere evidence in one case could be an instrument in another. Because of this, in the 1967 case of *Warden v. Hayden*, the Court overturned the mere evidence rule. Police had entered

Hayden's house, without a warrant, because a person who had robbed a taxi cab company had been observed running into the home. The police arrived on the scene and knocked on the door. Mrs. Hayden answered, and the police told her they believed a robber had entered her house and asked her permission to conduct a search. She allowed them to do so. Once inside, they found Mr. Hayden pretending to sleep. They also found a shotgun and a pistol hidden in the toilet tank, clothes in the basement that fit the description of those worn by the robber of the cab company, and ammunition for the guns hidden under Hayden's mattress and in a bureau. Hayden was arrested and, based on the evidence gathered in this warrantless search, was convicted. Hayden appealed to the Supreme Court, claiming that the mere evidence rule had been violated.

The Court, in an 8–1 decision, not only refused to overturn his conviction but overturned the mere evidence rule as well. Property wasn't the main concern of the Fourth Amendment, the Court said, but privacy. Further, the tests for determining what constituted "mere evidence" were impossible to keep consistent.

One effect of the reversal of the mere evidence rule was an erosion of the Fourth Amendment's protection of personal papers. Several decisions in the 1970s upheld the principle that a valid search warrant can be used to collect anything that might be considered evidence of a crime.

WARRANTLESS SEARCHES AND ARRESTS

The Fourth Amendment does not specifically state anything about arrests. It merely protects people from unreasonable searches and seizures. However, an arrest is, after all, a seizure: the seizure of a person. As such, Supreme Court decisions about the legality of arrests have been based on the Fourth Amendment.

That being said, the Supreme Court has not held arrests to the same standard it has held other searches and seizures. A warrantless arrest is legal under many more circumstances than a search or seizure of evidence. However, certain basic standards still apply.

Just as probable cause is required before a judge will grant a warrant, an officer who arrests somebody without a warrant must have probable cause to believe that he or she has committed a crime. As long as probable cause exists, an arrest without a warrant will generally be upheld.

Three separate important cases illustrate various aspects of the ability of government agents to make warrantless arrests: *United States v.*

A man is arrested in Aspen, Colorado, after a search of his person revealed he was in possession of illegal drugs (marijuana) and weapons (brass knuckles).

Watson (1976), *United States v. Santana* (1976), and *Payton v. New York* (1980).

UNITED STATES V. WATSON

The first of these cases involves the warrantless arrest of a suspect in a public place. A postal inspector saw a man believed to have stolen credit cards in a restaurant and arrested him. A search of the suspect's car found two stolen credit cards, which were used to convict him. The Supreme Court heard the case after a lower court had overturned the conviction on the basis of Watson's Fourth Amendment rights. The Supreme Court justices reinstated the conviction. The Court noted that laws specifically gave postal inspectors the right to perform warrantless arrests based on probable cause and that doing so in this case did not mean that government agents should not generally get a warrant when arresting someone in public.

UNITED STATES V. SANTANA

Also in 1976, the Court made a ruling about whether or not a warrantless arrest made inside a house was constitutional. In *United States v. Santana*, the police had received information that a person known as "Mom" Santana was in possession of marked money that had been used to buy drugs. When they approached her house, they saw her standing on the porch with a paper bag in her hands, at which point they rushed up, shouting, "Police!" She ran inside her house, and the police followed her and arrested her. Heroin was found in the bag she was carrying, and she had some of the marked money. During the trial process, however, she moved to have the heroin and money excluded on the grounds that her arrest was illegal, since her home had been entered without a warrant.

The Court disagreed. Santana had been outside the home, exposed to public view and scrutiny. Moreover, once she was outside and observed by the police, she could not then stop them from arresting her merely by going inside. The facts of the case gave the police enough probable cause to believe a crime had been committed.

PAYTON V. NEW YORK

In 1980, the Court ruled in *Payton v. New York* that the police or government agents cannot enter a home to arrest its occupant without a warrant or the consent of the occupant. The difference in the case seems to be that in Payton, the action did not begin outside the house. Rather, the police, believing Payton had murdered someone, went to his apartment to arrest him. When no one answered the door, they broke it down and used evidence found inside to convict him. In a narrow 5–4 decision, the Court found this kind of entry to be unconstitutional and beyond the scope of the police's right to make warrantless arrests.

SEARCH AND SEIZURE ON THE STREET: FRISKING

"Frisking" refers to the practice of a police officer stopping a suspicious person and searching him or her for weapons. The Supreme Court has upheld this as a reasonable search under the Fourth Amendment.

One of the most important decisions in this area was the 1968 case of *Terry v. Ohio*. In this case, the

Los Angeles police officers frisk two residents of a public housing complex controlled by members of the Bloods gang.

Court found that the police must have some ability to search suspects for weapons, if only for their own protection. The police need not have enough probable cause to arrest the person, just enough to believe that he or she might be armed. A case decided at the same time, *Sibron v. New York*, however, demonstrated the limits of this frisking. In the *Terry* case, the officer had patted down the suspect and, feeling a suspicious object, then reached inside the suspect's pockets, where he found a weapon. In *Sibron*, however, the officer had immediately searched the suspect's pockets, without patting him down first.

In 1993, this ruling was expanded to include any "contraband" (things that people are prohibited by law from possessing, such as illegal drugs) provided that the officer can clearly feel the material during the frisking. This is a sort of "plain feel" exemption that complements the more basic "plain view" exemption.

JUSTIFICATIONS FOR SEARCHES DURING ARRESTS

At the time of a person's arrest, the police have the ability to search the person and the area around him or her without a warrant. There are three basic reasons for this, all of which, in the eyes of the Supreme Court, have elevated the public good over the rights of the person being arrested: the chance that the person might be concealing weapons, which could endanger the officers arresting him or her; the need to prevent the escape of the person; and the need to avoid the destruction of evidence.

This custom has a long history, and the Court has not changed it, for the reasons listed above. However, for the search to be considered valid, the arrest itself must have been valid independent of any items discovered during the search.

AN INCREASE IN FRISKING AND RACIAL PROFILING

Following the release of stop-and-frisk statistics for April–June 2010 in New York City, the Center for Constitutional Rights (CCR) expressed its alarm over what it saw as a rising tide of Fourth Amendment violations, particularly among ethnic and racial minorities, by law enforcement. The New York Police Department statistics were released to the public by court order. They revealed a 21 percent increase in such warrantless street searches over the same period in 2009, with over a half a million New Yorkers being stopped and frisked. Eighty-eight percent of those who were frisked were African American or Hispanic, but these groups represent only about one-quarter of the city's population. Only 1.3 percent of these stops resulted in the discovery of a weapon, and only 6 percent resulted in arrests. Meanwhile, according to CCR, many schoolchildren's daily experience includes a stop-and-frisk by the police.

CCR claims that these police tactics—stop-and-frisking and racial profiling—in addition to violating the fundamental rights and protections of the Fourth and Fourteenth amendments and the Civil Rights Act of 1964, also promote distrust of law enforcement within minority communities, ultimately making the police department's work more difficult and dangerous.

The Center for Constitutional Rights is dedicated to advancing and protecting the rights guaranteed by the U.S. Constitution and the Universal Declaration of Human Rights. Founded in 1966 by attorneys who represented civil rights movements in the South, CCR is a nonprofit legal and educational organization committed to the creative use of law as a positive force for social change.

Even so, this ability of the police is quite broad and rather undefined. What exactly were the limits to the police's power to search a person and, more important, the area he or she was in—especially if it was his or her home or office? At what point does such a search become unreasonable?

HARRIS V. UNITED STATES

One of the first major cases to try and fix these limits was *Harris v. United States* (1947). In this case, the Federal Bureau of Investigation (FBI) had arrested a man for mail fraud in his home and then searched his entire apartment without a warrant. The search took five hours to complete and did not uncover any evidence of mail fraud. Several draft cards that had been stolen were found, however, and Harris was convicted for their possession.

His appeal to the Supreme Court on the grounds that his Fourth Amendment rights had been infringed was rejected. Since Harris had been in control of his apartment, the Court concluded that the agents were justified in searching it. The decision was only 5–4, and Justice Murphy bitterly noted in his dissenting opinion that the Court had in effect revived the hated general warrant of colonial days.

TRUPIANO V. UNITED STATES

The next year, however, the case of *Trupiano v. United States* resulted in some limitations on the ability of government agents to perform searches and seizures without warrants. In this case, federal agents had, without a warrant, arrested several men they had seen operating an illegal alcohol still. They had also then seized the still. The Court found that while the agents had probable cause to make the arrest, they did not have the right to seize the still without a warrant. The still was not a danger to their safety, nor was it apparently in danger of being destroyed. There was nothing to prevent them from getting a warrant, Justice Murphy (writing for the majority this time) noted, except their "indifference to the legal process...which the Constitution contemplated." There had to be some dividing line between the circumstances that required the government to seize items without a warrant at the time of arrest and when they were required to first obtain a warrant, or else the Fourth Amendment would have no meaning. Another decision made that year made it clear that unless the officers were responding to an emergency, there had to be exceptional, exigent—requiring immediate action—circumstances for a warrantless search to be valid.

UNITED STATES V. RABINOWITZ

Shortly thereafter, though, the Court made yet another ruling that changed the *Trupiano* ruling that

A woman who had been loitering outside the U.S. Capitol building is detained and searched by Capitol police.

a warrant be obtained whenever doing so was practical. In *United States v. Rabinowitz*, the Court ruled that the search of the desk, file cabinets, and safe of a person who had been arrested on a valid arrest warrant in his one-room office was not unreasonable. Furthermore, it held that the failure of the government to obtain a search warrant even though they had time to do so did not make the search invalid. Thus, in overturning the "practicability" restriction on warrantless searches in the *Trupiano* ruling, the Court found that deciding whether or not a search was unreasonable when conducted without a warrant did not depend on whether or not getting a search warrant was reasonable, but whether the search itself was reasonable. This could be determined only by considering the "total atmosphere" of the case. Determining exactly what the "total atmosphere" of a case meant and which circumstances would permit a warrantless search proved to be extremely difficult, and in 1969 the Court changed its position again in the case of *Chimel v. California.*

In this case, police officers had come to the house of a man with a warrant for his arrest on burglary charges. He was not home, but his wife let them in and they waited for him to return. When he did, they arrested him and then asked if they could search his house. Although he refused to give his permission, the officers searched the entire building for nearly an hour and seized many items that were used to convict him at trial.

In reversing his conviction, the Court found that while the police certainly had a right to search both the person they had arrested and the area around him or her, the search of an entire house without a search warrant was unreasonable. Only the area under the immediate control of the person they were arresting could be considered reasonable, as this was the zone where he or she might grab a weapon or try to destroy evidence. In other cases, a search warrant would have to be obtained. In doing so, they thus overturned not only *Rabinowitz*, but *Harris* as well, establishing a new standard of reasonableness that still stands today.

OTHER IMPORTANT SEARCH AND ARREST PRECEDENTS

Subsequent decisions have reinforced this standard. In 1970, the Court decided that arresting a person on the street for a drug offense did not justify a search of his house without a warrant. And in 1971, the case of *Coolidge v. New Hampshire* found that even if the police arrest a suspect inside his house, it was not reasonable for them to search a car that was in the suspect's driveway.

Another case worth noting combined both the rights of officers to search a car without a warrant and the search of an individual without a warrant. In *United States v. Robinson*, the Court had to decide on the admissibility of drug evidence that had been discovered when an officer frisked a suspect after stopping his car. However, the police had not stopped the car because they suspected the driver of having committed a drug offense but because he was suspected of driving with a revoked license. The Court ruled, however, that since searching the suspect, even for a traffic violation, was reasonable, the drug evidence discovered by this search was reasonable as well.

A FLAWED SEARCH WARRANT AND AN ARREST BASED UPON DISPUTED EVIDENCE

An even more complicated case of a warrantless search of a suspect's car and home occurred in 2010. Robert Starnes Jr., on parole for an earlier crime, became the leading suspect in the June 21, 2010, robbery of a bank in Sheffield Lake, Ohio. In Ohio, law enforcement agents are permitted to conduct searches of parolees' homes and vehicles without warrants. Yet at the time of the search of Starnes's apartment and car, a judge had actually removed him from parole since Starnes had accepted a plea deal in the earlier case. The state refused to accept this court order—though they never actually appealed the order—and continued to treat Starnes as a parolee for the purposes of the search warrant.

Because bank robbery is a federal offense, agents of the FBI descended upon Starnes's apartment to conduct a search. Though not requiring a warrant according to the state of Ohio, FBI agents nevertheless received signed consent from Starnes's wife to search their apartment. However, Starnes's wife was hand-cuffed and forced to the floor when the FBI arrived and arrested Starnes. So her subsequent consent to the search could be viewed as made under duress. During the search, the agents found notebook paper and handwriting similar to the hold-up note handed to a bank teller, a BB gun that had been shown to the teller during the robbery, and a red, white, and blue bandanna similar to one worn during the robbery. Though the FBI agents claimed they didn't search Starnes's car, they nevertheless removed from it a camouflage baseball cap similar to that worn by the bank robber.

Lawyers for Starnes argued in U.S. District Court that the evidence gathered from his apartment and car should be declared inadmissible and thrown out. Federal prosecutors wanted to use the evidence to try Starnes on robbery charges for the Sheffield Lake robbery as well as two other Ohio bank robberies that occurred in June and July of 2010. The prosecutors insisted that the evidence was both permissible and legally gathered, despite the lack of a warrant and the questionable consent given by Starnes's wife. The federal courts will ultimately decide if law enforcement operated within constitutional bounds or violated Starnes's Fourth Amendment rights.

CHAPTER 7

CAR SEARCHES

When the Fourth Amendment was written, the primary means of transportation was riding a horse or a horse-drawn wagon, or by sailing ship. However, in the early twentieth century, a new form of transportation became overwhelmingly common: the automobile.

Cars present an interesting challenge to interpretations of the Fourth Amendment. On the one hand, they are hardly either the "person" or "house" of a citizen, so they do not seem to be covered by the Fourth Amendment. However, it is undeniable that many people view their cars as part of their personal space, much like their homes, containing items of a personal nature. Since 1925, the Supreme Court has had to weigh both these concerns carefully in defining the degree to which the Fourth Amendment protects a person's automobile.

CARROLL V. UNITED STATES

The first case to really address the issues involved in warrantless searches of automobiles was *Carroll v. United States* (1925), decided during Prohibition, when the federal government enforced the Eighteenth Amendment's ban on manufacturing, selling, or transporting alcoholic beverages. George Carroll had been arrested and convicted of transporting liquor on the basis of evidence that had been taken from his car, without a search warrant, by federal agents.

The Court's decision provided the basic framework for all subsequent decisions. Since the Fourth Amendment had been ratified, the Court noted, a fundamental difference had been recognized between a search of a building or other structure and the search of a wagon or a boat. Simply put, in the latter case, there was a very real danger that the evidence would be moved out of the jurisdiction of the officers during the time it took to get a search warrant. The public's interest in obtaining evidence of criminal activity outweighed any expectation of privacy in this case.

By 1949, the precise breadth of this exception to the Fourth Amendment's warrant requirement had been spelled out. The police were allowed to search a parked car, because a suspect might move it without their knowledge, for example. The basic rule, which remains in place, is that the police have the right to make a warrantless search whenever they have probable cause that the car has been involved in an illegal activity. Without probable cause, however, the search would be considered unreasonable, and the Court

A police search warrant for the offices of Tha Row Records (formerly Death Row Records), a rap music label, also included the vehicles of label executives.

has repeatedly thrown out evidence stemming from such searches.

AUTOMOBILE SEARCHES IN THE WAKE OF BOTH THE *MAPP* AND *CARROLL* DECISIONS

Since *Mapp v. Ohio* "incorporated" the Fourth Amendment, the Supreme Court's decisions have amounted to a national evidence policy, affecting not only federal agents but state and city police as well.

The Court has remained true to the ruling of *Carroll v. United States* and has allowed police broad exceptions to the warrant requirement when searching cars.

For example, the Court has allowed the police to take paint samples from a car parked in a public parking lot. It has also not required that the police obtain a warrant to search a car that they have impounded, even up to a week later.

However, a series of rulings in the 1970s and early 1980s created a confusing system of exceptions to the warrant requirement that were sometimes apparently contradictory to each other. The Court has with some difficulty tried to straighten out these concerns to make a consistent policy.

SEARCHING PASSENGERS: *RAKAS V. ILLINOIS*

A 1978 case addressed the Fourth Amendment concerns of passengers in a car that the police decided to search. In *Rakas v. Illinois*, the Court had to decide if evidence uncovered by the police during a warrantless search of a car could be used against people who were only riding in the car.

The Court decided that it could. The search itself had been reasonable and proper: the police had probable cause because the car matched the description of a car used as the getaway vehicle in a robbery that had taken place in the area. Furthermore, the Fourth Amendment protected only unreasonable searches of a person's body or property. If the evidence being used against a person had been found on another person's "premises or property," their Fourth Amendment rights had not been violated. Since none of the passengers claimed to own either the car or the items that were seized by the police, the Fourth Amendment did not apply.

The decision in this case was arrived at by a 5–4 vote and was sharply criticized by the dissenting justices for making property rights more important than privacy rights.

RESTRICTING AUTOMOBILE SEARCHES

The minority's concern in *Rakas v. Illinois* was that, as Justice White put it, "open season" would be declared for all searches of automobiles. However, this seemed to be disproved by two further rulings.

The first came only four months after *Rakas*. In *Delaware v. Prouse*, the Court voted 8–1 to find that the police practice of randomly stopping motorists to check their licenses and registrations violated the Fourth Amendment because it did not meet the probable cause test. In the case, Prouse had been stopped by a Delaware patrolman, but only to check his license and registration; he had not broken any traffic laws. When the patrolman approached his car, however, he smelled marijuana smoke and, looking in, saw marijuana lying in plain view on the floor of the car. Prouse was arrested but during a trial hearing asked for the evidence seized to be suppressed under his Fourth Amendment rights. The case eventually reached the Supreme Court, which agreed with Prouse. Any searches and seizures conducted during a random stoppage without probable cause of a specific crime could not be admitted as evidence. This case also involved issues of the "plain view" exceptions, which require the officer to be conducting a legal search—which was not the case here.

Then, in 1981, the Court restricted automobile searches even further. Their ruling in the case of *Robbins v. California* found that in order to search a closed container within a car, such as a piece of luggage, the police must get a warrant, even if their search was otherwise reasonable. This protection, however, was to be short-lived.

PROBABLE CAUSE: UNITED STATES V. ROSS

On November 27, 1978, District of Columbia police had been given a tip from an informant that illegal drugs were being sold from a parked car. Although the police were told the location of the car, when they arrived on the scene they did not see anybody in the area and left. Shortly thereafter, they returned to see the car being driven off. They followed the car after noticing that the person driving it matched the description they had been given of the person suspected of selling illegal drugs. They stopped the car and found a pistol inside the glove compartment. One officer then opened the trunk of the car and found a closed paper bag that, when he opened it, was found to contain heroin. The police arrested the man, Ross, and impounded the car. A search done while the car was impounded also turned up a closed leather pouch that contained a few thousand dollars.

On the basis of this evidence, Ross was convicted. The U.S. Court of Appeals, however, reversed the conviction under the *Robbins* decision, and the United States government (the case took place in the District of Columbia, which is governed directly by the federal government) appealed the case to the Supreme Court.

The Court not only reinstated Ross's conviction but also disposed of the rationale of the *Robbins* case. The limiting factor of any reasonable search, whether conducted with or without a warrant, was not the containers within which evidence was concealed, but probable cause. If there was probable cause to believe that the trunk of a car—as there seemed to be in this case—contained evidence of a crime, the police were justified in searching the trunk and any containers inside it. The Court decided this because the police would have been justified in searching, with a warrant, inside of jars if a place was suspected of being a drug lab. There was no fundamental difference between the scope of a warrantless search and one conducted with a warrant, provided that each one was reasonable. And, since the Court judged that the search in this case was reasonable, the evidence uncovered by the police was admissible.

OTHER IMPORTANT CAR SEARCH PRECEDENTS

Since the *Ross* case, the Court has generally continued to expand the police's ability to make warrantless searches of automobiles.

In 1991, the case of *California v. Acevedo*, for example, ruled that the police were authorized to search an entire car without a warrant, including all closed containers inside it, even if they had probable cause to think that just one of the containers held evidence.

Michigan v. Sitz, decided in 1990, found that the police had a right to set up checkpoints to see if people were driving while drunk and to randomly search cars at those checkpoints. The judgment of the Court was that the inconvenience that the checkpoints created was only slight, but they did much to discourage drunk driving.

Police officers in San Bruno, California, stop cars, question drivers, and peer inside cars at a DUI checkpoint.

In 1985, the Court ruled that a mobile home still fell under the exceptions given to regular cars. In *California v. Carney*, the police had, without a warrant, searched the mobile home of a person suspected of giving boys marijuana in exchange for sex, and they discovered evidence of drug use that was used to convict the owner of the mobile home. The Court upheld the reasonableness of their search because the mobile home was fully capable of being driven and was located in a public space, a parking lot in downtown San Diego. However, the Court took pains to note that both these qualifications had to be present in order for a mobile home to be considered an automobile and not a home deserving the protection of the Fourth Amendment.

In 1996, the Court ruled that even if the police have another crime in mind, they are authorized to stop a car that has violated a traffic law and search it without a warrant. The case, *Whren v. United States*, involved two black men who had been pulled over on a minor traffic complaint and searched. They were found to have crack cocaine with them. Their lawyers argued, however, that if the police officer's actions were deemed acceptable then in the future the police would simply follow people they suspected of committing more serious crimes until they violated a traffic law—in violation of the probable cause limitation of the Fourth Amendment. But the Court rejected this argument because it claimed that the police had the right to pull over and search people who broke the traffic laws, even if the police had "bigger game" on their minds. This thinking has been criticized in light of the controversial allegations of racial profiling, which involves using a person's ethnicity when determining whether to make a search or arrest.

Arrest at a Pizzeria

Sometimes, evidence of a new crime can be uncovered when a suspect is being arrested for an older crime. On March 13, 2009, Indiana State Police officers

FAILING TO ASK PERMISSION

Situations in which evidence of a crime is discovered by accident pose special challenges to Fourth Amendment law and its interpretation. Following a three-car accident in Coralville, Iowa, one of the drivers involved, Tara Garrison, complained to a police officer of pain. The police officer sent her to a nearby ambulance. A second police officer was instructed to gather Garrison's insurance, license, and registration information.

Since Garrison was being treated in the ambulance, the officer entered her car without permission and searched the glove compartment and center console to look for the license, insurance, and registration information. In the center console, he found a pill bottle stuffed with a plastic baggie containing marijuana and a glass pipe. Garrison later admitted to having smoked marijuana the day before and agreed to turn herself in at a later date. She was charged with possession of a controlled substance.

Garrison and her lawyers sought for the suppression of the evidence, saying it had been obtained through an illegal warrantless search and seizure that violated both state and federal constitutional protections. The court, however, found that this search and seizure was justified under a "community caretaking" exception to warrant requirements. This exception permits a warrantless search of an automobile for the protection of the public and in the interests of public safety, rather than for the detection, investigation, or acquisition of evidence relating to the violation of a criminal statute. Garrison was found guilty and sentenced.

When this decision was appealed to Iowa's Court of Appeals in 2010, however, the judges found in favor of Garrison. They disagreed with the lower

Circuit Court's conclusion that the police officer's search of the car was a legitimate community caretaker activity. When the officers arrived on the scene, the three cars involved in the accident had already been pulled off to the side of the road and the fire department was handling traffic control, so public safety had been secured. The judges also pointed out that the second officer did not ask Garrison for license, registration, and insurance information or for permission to enter her car to search for these. He simply began searching for them under the direction of the first officer.

Given these circumstances, the Iowa Court of Appeals found both that the community caretaking exception didn't apply here and that there was no reason for a warrantless search to be conducted since Garrison was still at the accident site and lucid and could produce the desired information if she had only been asked for it.

parked across the street from a pizza restaurant where James Hobbs, a man they were seeking to serve with an arrest warrant, was believed to work. The officers identified the suspect when he left the pizzeria and placed an object in his car. The police got out of their patrol car to arrest Hobbs, but traffic prevented them from crossing the street quickly, and Hobbs had reentered the building by the time they reached his car.

The officers entered the pizzeria and arrested Hobbs. They asked permission to search his car, which Hobbs

An explosives-sniffing dog searches a car in Washington, D.C., as part of an antiterrorist domestic security operation. Drug-sniffing dogs are also used by police to search individuals, vehicles, and luggage for illegal drugs.

refused to give. A drug-sniffing dog was then called in. The dog quickly reacted to the scent of something in the car, and the officers felt this gave them probable cause to execute a warrantless search of Hobbs's car. Upon entering the vehicle, the officers found a cooler containing two scales (used to weigh and measure out drugs), plastic sandwich bags (used to parcel out individual quantities of drugs for sale), rolling papers (to make marijuana cigarettes), and marijuana.

Hobbs was charged with possession of marijuana and drug paraphernalia. The trial court, however, found that the evidence had been seized illegally. Though the drug-sniffing dog's reaction did provide probable cause for a search warrant request, it did not justify a warrantless search. The court ordered that the evidence be excluded and Hobbs be released on the drug charges. The state of Indiana appealed the case, and the Court of Appeals overturned the trial court's decision. It claimed that the dog's response did provide probable cause for a warrantless search, and therefore no Fourth Amendment rights were violated. The suspect was already under arrest, and the dog's reaction indicated a strong likelihood that a controlled substance was present in Hobbs's car. The case was then appealed again, this time to the Indiana Supreme Court.

The state supreme court justices considered whether the warrantless search of Hobbs's car was covered under one of the exceptions to search and seizure

Fourth Amendment protections. One of these exceptions is known as the "search incident to arrest exception." This exception allows searches and seizures during arrests of "an area into which an arrestee might reach" and hide evidence or weapons. It also allows searches if there is a danger that evidence will be destroyed or officer safety is at risk. The Indiana Supreme Court found that this exception did not apply in the Hobbs case. He had already been successfully arrested and secured, so officer safety was not at risk. Hobbs was also arrested away from his car, so he wasn't in a position to stash evidence in it. Most important, he was arrested for an earlier crime, one that was irrelevant to any evidence that might be sought and discovered in his car at the moment of arrest.

There is another exception under which warrantless searches and seizures are permitted however—the so-called "automobile exception." This exception allows police to search a vehicle without obtaining a warrant if they have probable cause to believe evidence of a crime will be found in the vehicle, especially when that vehicle is located in a public area.

Under this criteria, the Indiana Supreme Court found that the officers did indeed have probable cause for a warrantless search based upon their own observations of the suspect placing an object in his car and the drug-sniffing dog's reaction.

SEARCHES ACROSS BORDERS, THROUGH FIELDS, AND OF THE BODY

T his chapter will investigate some of the lesser-known areas of Fourth Amendment rights, such as searches at the border and in open fields.

CHAPTER 8

SEARCHES AT OR NEAR BORDER CROSSINGS

In general, the Court has found that the Fourth Amendment protections apply to searches of cars conducted near the border. It has, however, found certain important exceptions.

The first major case in this area was the 1973 decision in *Almeida-Sanchez v. United States*. The defendant in this case had been stopped by a roving patrol of the United States Border Patrol while driving on a highway in California some 20 miles (32 kilometers) from the border. The Border Patrol had been authorized by federal law to look for illegal aliens anywhere within 100 miles (161 km) of the U.S. border.

Border Patrol agents west of Tucson, Arizona, search a van for illegal drugs.

Acting without a search warrant, the agents searched the defendant's car and found marijuana in it. He was arrested and convicted of illegally transporting marijuana across the border. His appeal ended up in the Supreme Court, which reversed his conviction. While the government clearly had the right to exclude aliens from the country, and this right included searches at the border, or where a "functional" border might exist, searching Almeida-Sanchez's car 20 miles (32 km) from the border was wholly unreasonable.

Two years later, the Court's ruling in *United States v. Ortiz* went even further. The Court found that searches conducted at an official checkpoint that was 66 miles (106 km) from the border, at the discretion of the officers and without probable cause, were also unreasonable. A separate ruling in *United States v. Brignoni-Ponce*, issued that same day ruled that probable cause did not include the fact that the occupants of a car "appeared to be" Mexican. However, the Court specifically left open the matter of stopping a car merely to question its occupants. Also, the *Brignoni-Ponce* decision stated that the full standard of probable cause did not need to be fulfilled when the Border Patrol stopped people to question them as to whether or not they were aliens.

In 1976, the Court found that nonintrusive visual searches of cars conducted at a border checkpoint did not violate the Fourth Amendment. The case, *United States v. Martinez-Fuerte*, involved the practice of slowing traffic down at the border checkpoint and then sending cars the Border Patrol had picked out to a separate area, where their occupants were questioned. Since the intrusion was much less severe than the searches conducted in the other rulings, they did not violate Fourth Amendment standards.

In an interesting aside, in 1990 the Court found, in *United States v. Verdugo-Urquidez*, that U.S. agents could search a foreigner without a warrant while they were in a foreign country. The Fourth Amendment protections did not apply to those not within the

national "community" or who had developed suffi-
cient "connection" to that community.

Curtilage: Extending the Parameters of "Home"

The law has long recognized that a person's "home"
can entail more than just the physical building he or
she lives in. For example, a person's porch or even her
backyard is not only part of the grounds where she
lives but can also be considered part of the "home"
for Fourth Amendment purposes. In other words,
before the area can be searched, the government must
acquire a search warrant. These outlying areas are
known in legal terms as the "curtilage." In 1984, the
Court was asked to rule how far the curtilage
extended in *Oliver v. United States*.

Kentucky State Police agents had received a tip
that marijuana was being grown on Oliver's farm.
They went to the farm and found a footpath leading
beyond a locked gate that had a "No Trespassing"
sign on it. At the end of the path, nearly a mile from
Oliver's house, was a field of marijuana. Oliver was
arrested, but before the trial began, he moved that the
"evidence" of the field's existence be suppressed. The
case eventually was appealed to the Supreme Court.

In 1924, in *Hester v. United States*, the Court had
ruled that open fields, such as pastures and vacant lots,

A special agent of the Campaign Against Marijuana Planting (CAMP) flies over Annapolis, California, in a helicopter searching for marijuana "gardens" in advance of a raid.

were not protected by the Fourth Amendment. They upheld this doctrine in the *Oliver* case as well. Although in this case the field was remote and well hidden from the public view, the issue was not whether or not the area was "private," but rather if the government's action violated the "personal and societal values protected by the Fourth Amendment." In this case, they did not. The field was too far removed from Oliver's house to be considered part of his curtilage, and the evidence was allowed to stand.

THE ROBERTS COURT AND SEARCH AND SEIZURE

In 2009, the Supreme Court, led by Chief Justice John Roberts, voted 5–4 to uphold the admissibility of evidence gathered via a faulty arrest warrant. The suspect, Bennie Dean Herring, had arrived at the Coffee County Sheriff's Department in Alabama to check on his pickup truck, which had been impounded. A police officer asked a clerk to check for any outstanding warrants that might have been issued for Herring. The clerk turned up an outstanding arrest warrant. This prompted the police officer to arrest Herring and search his truck. In the meantime, the clerk discovered that the arrest warrant had actually been recalled five months earlier. Before the police officer could be alerted to this fact, however, he had searched Herring's vehicle and found guns and methamphetamines. Herring was charged with weapons and drug offenses and was convicted and sentenced to twenty-seven months in federal prison. Herring appealed his case several times, eventually reaching the Supreme Court. In each appeal, Herring claimed that his arrest was unlawful because it was set in motion by an invalid warrant and the drug and firearms evidence should have been suppressed based on the exclusionary rule. Yet the Supreme Court found that when police mistakes that result in unlawful searches are due to "isolated negligence" rather than "systemic error" or "reckless disregard" of constitutional requirements, the exclusionary rule does not apply. In essence, the police officer had been acting in good faith when he arrested Herring and searched his vehicle.

Also in 2009, however, the Roberts Court limited law enforcement's ability to engage in a warrantless search of a suspect's vehicle without probable cause. While staking out a suspected drug den in Tucson, Arizona, police officers observed Rodney Gant, a drug suspect, drive up to the house and exit his vehicle. Having looked up Gant in their computer system, the officers discovered he had an outstanding warrant for driving with a suspended license. Using this warrant, the officers arrested Gant and searched his car, finding a gun and cocaine. Gant and his lawyers argued that this was an illegal search, and the Supreme Court agreed. Any searches made during an arrest are meant to ensure officer safety and the preservation of evidence. In this case, Gant was already handcuffed and sitting in a patrol car. He posed no threat to the officers or to any evidence that may have been in his car. Most important, the arrest warrant for driving with a suspended license had nothing to do with suspected drug activity, so there was no probable cause linking the outstanding arrest warrant and the vehicle search conducted by police. The Supreme Court argued that after Gant's arrest, the police should have sought a separate search warrant, based upon the probable cause provided by the suspect's visiting of a known drug den. Many court observers regard this as a rare victory for the Fourth Amendment in the Roberts Court.

Since the *Oliver* ruling, the Court has allowed further warrantless searches even within the curtilage of a home. In *California v. Ciraolo* (1986), it ruled that the way in which the police obtained evidence that the defendant was growing marijuana in his backyard was admissible. The ruling was based on the fact that the police, by flying over the man's backyard, had only observed what anyone flying across the land could have observed; therefore, there could not be a reasonable expectation of privacy.

Further rulings have upheld this doctrine, even when the police use special cameras capable of taking pictures at a distance from which the details would not be visible to the naked eye. The "open fields" doctrine has also justified police searches of garbage that has been left out in the street for collection, based on the idea that there can be no reasonable expectation of privacy for discarded materials left in public view. And in one case, the Court ruled that shredding a document before throwing it away did not create an expectation of privacy—it merely underestimated how diligent the federal agents who managed to piece the document together, strip by strip, could be.

BODY SEARCHES

The Court has had to rule at various times about searches of a person's clothing, for example in *Terry v. Ohio* (see chapter 6). However, what protection does a person have against searches of his or her body? And what about fingerprints or blood samples? Does collecting samples of either of these constitute a search?

The basic principle in these cases was set out by Justice Oliver Wendell Holmes Jr. in the 1910 case of *Holt v. United States*. In his decision, Holmes ruled that a person's body need not be excluded as evidence under the Fourth Amendment. Furthermore, characteristics of a public nature—such as fingerprints—could be "seized" by the government and used as evidence without violating the Fifth Amendment's protection from self-incrimination.

This doctrine has been used to allow the collection of voice samples, without a warrant, to identify a suspect. It similarly allows the use of handwriting samples; since a person's handwriting is knowingly exposed to the public every day, no expectation of privacy exists. Likewise, fingerprints, which are left on every physical object we touch, are allowed to be collected by the government without a warrant.

However, the Court has ruled that collecting evidence from certain bodily traits is intrusive enough to be considered a search under the Fourth Amendment. For example, while a person's fingerprints are a kind of "public statement" not protected by the Fourth Amendment, scraping under a person's fingernails to

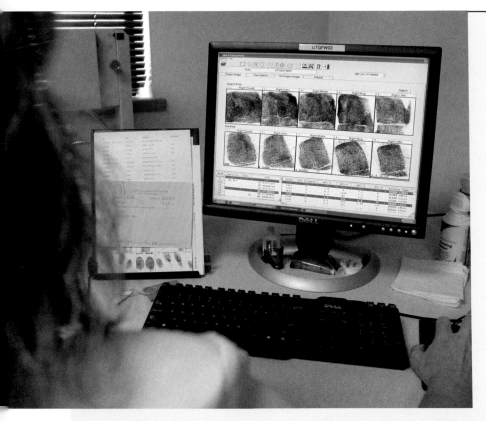

A set of fingerprints is compared with those in a database at the Bureau of Criminal Identification in Kearns, Utah, in order to come up with a match and identify the perpetrator of a crime.

find evidence of a crime is considered a search and requires a warrant. Since 1966, the Court has also considered blood tests to be searches. Under this logic, the Court refused to allow the state of Virginia to remove a bullet from the chest of a man who might have been wounded during a robbery. Although the bullet might prove that he was guilty, the Court found that drugging a citizen not yet convicted of a crime and performing surgery on him was too severe an invasion of privacy to be allowed.

Drug testing has also raised Fourth Amendment issues. Both the taking of urine samples and breath testing have been deemed searches by the Court. Breath tests require that air be expelled from deep within the lungs, which was close enough to a blood test in the Court's eyes. And while urine tests would seem to involve only material that has left the body, the fact that chemical analysis of it could reveal many facts about a person made it invasive enough, in the Court's eyes, to qualify it as a search requiring a warrant.

WIRETAPPING AND ELECTRONIC SURVEILLANCE

When the Fourth Amendment was ratified, the primary means of communication over distance in the United States was the written letter, which was clearly protected as a person's "papers." Future inventions such as the telegraph, telephone, and radio were obviously beyond the ability of the Founders to predict, not to mention computers, smartphones, cyberspace, blogs, tweets, and other forms of digital communication. At the start of the twentieth century, however, these technologies were so prevalent that constitutional questions about them finally had to be resolved by the Supreme Court.

The Court has been faced with two basic kinds of electronic surveillance: wiretapping, which is the use of equipment to listen in on private telephone calls, and the use of electronic "bugs" to listen in on private conversations. Both kinds of surveillance are the same in that the people who are being overheard do not know that they are being monitored.

OLMSTEAD V. UNITED STATES

The first Supreme Court case involving electronic surveillance of any kind was the 1928

Protesters in Chicago, Illinois, protest the federal government's domestic wiretapping program, instituted by President George W. Bush in the wake of the 9/11 terrorist attacks.

case of *Olmstead v. United States*. This controversial 5–4 decision caused severe disagreement within the Court itself.

The case involved the use of wiretaps by federal agents to gather evidence about a bootlegging ring. This evidence was used to convict the members of the ring, who had then appealed, claiming that their Fourth Amendment rights had been violated by the agents. Chief Justice (and former president) William Howard Taft disagreed. The Fourth Amendment, he claimed, protected only physical things, such as papers or contraband. The agents, by merely listening in on conversations, had neither performed a search nor seized any evidence. Therefore, the Fourth Amendment protections did not apply, although Congress could, of course, pass laws forbidding agents to use wiretaps.

Both Justice Oliver Wendell Holmes Jr. and Louis Brandeis dissented vigorously with the decision. Both noted that wiretapping was already illegal under federal law for private individuals to perform; surely the government should not be allowed to commit a crime, even if it was done to convict a criminal. Justice Brandeis further argued that science and technology were continuing to advance and that future innovations might be able to accomplish far greater invasions of privacy than merely listening in on phone conversations. Yet under this decision, the Fourth Amendment would not protect people from such invasions of privacy; without the protection of that amendment, the government would not even need a warrant to listen in on any citizen, regardless of whether or not he or she was suspected of committing a crime.

THE FEDERAL COMMUNICATIONS ACT AND RESTRICTIONS UPON WIRETAPPING

Congress took Chief Justice Taft's suggestion that they could pass legislation to prohibit wiretapping by federal agents to heart. In 1934, they passed the Federal Communications Act, which prohibited anyone not "authorized" by the sender of a communication from revealing its meaning or existence, which boiled down to a strict prohibition against using eavesdropped information. The Court came to this interpretation in *Nardone v. United States* (1937), which found that federal agents, and any other persons, were forbidden to use wiretaps to intercept telephone calls. By 1939, the Court had forbidden the use of any evidence obtained either directly or indirectly from wiretaps.

During World War II, when (rightly or wrongly) issues of national security took precedence in the minds of many, the Court retreated somewhat from the position of forbidding all evidence derived from wiretaps. In the cases of *Goldstein v. United States* and *Goldman v. United States*, both decided in 1942, the Court allowed the use of some evidence acquired by electronic surveillance. In the *Goldstein* case, the Court allowed the use of evidence derived from wiretapped conversations provided it was about a person who was not a part of the telephone conversation. And in *Goldman*, the Court decided that evidence obtained from a hidden electronic "bug" did not violate the Communications Act. The Court still operated under the *Olmstead* ruling, so the Fourth Amendment could not be considered in this decision.

In *Silverman v. United States* (1961), however, the Court disallowed evidence that had been collected with an electronic bug. The important factor in this case was that the bug had been physically driven into a wall. This was judged to be intrusive by the Court and set the stage for the much more dramatic decision in *Katz v. United States*.

PRIVACY IN PUBLIC: *KATZ v. UNITED STATES*

Charles Katz had been indicted in federal court for eight counts of operating an illegal bookmaking (gambling) ring. The evidence against him had been gathered in a highly creative fashion: rather than bugging his office or tapping his phone, the federal agents had placed a listening device on the outside of a public telephone booth. This had allowed them to eavesdrop on Katz's conversations. Because the bug was in a public location, and because it did not actually penetrate the wall of the phone booth, under previous rulings it would seem that the use of evidence obtained with it would be legal under the Fourth Amendment.

When the Court heard Katz's appeal in 1967, however, it disagreed. By closing the door to the phone booth, Katz had created a space where he had every expectation of privacy. This was the crucial issue, not whether or not the bug actually penetrated the wall of the booth.

The Court then discredited the idea that electronic eavesdropping did not constitute a search. Declaring that the Fourth Amendment protected only property and not privacy had been discredited, so the Court ruled that such eavesdropping was in fact a constitutional search. As such, it fell under the guidelines of the Fourth Amendment and the exclusionary rule, including the need to obtain a warrant from a neutral magistrate after demonstrating probable cause to be valid.

THE CRIME CONTROL AND SAFE STREETS ACT AND CHALLENGES TO IT

In 1969, the Court further ruled that defendants whose Fourth Amendment rights had been violated by electronic surveillance had to be presented with all the information collected against them. They could then challenge the parts of the evidence that the government was going to use to prosecute them. In many cases, this resulted in the government dropping charges against suspects, out of concern that handing over this information would reveal too much information on the methods the government had used to eavesdrop.

Congress had by that time passed the 1968 Crime Control and Safe Streets Act. This law tried to create

Agents gather information and intelligence at the Threat Operations Center, part of the National Security Agency, in Fort Meade, Maryland. The center is part of the federal government's domestic surveillance program.

guidelines for government officials that would satisfy the requirements of the *Katz* ruling. Now, in order for agents to begin electronic surveillance, they first had to get the approval of the Justice Department and then a warrant from a federal judge.

This act came into question in 1972, when the Court was asked to decide whether or not the president had an exception to the normal Fourth Amendment procedures. In *United States v. United States District Court*, the Court was asked to judge whether or not a warrantless wiretapping ordered by the president could be considered legal.

The case involved a man named Lawrence Plamondon, who was accused of having attempted to blow up the Central Intelligence Agency's (CIA) office in Ann Arbor, Michigan. He moved to have the government disclose whether or not it had used wiretapping to gather evidence against him. The government admitted that it had done so, without a warrant, but claimed that the Crime Control Act of 1969 permitted the president to order such a wiretap when national security demanded it. A district court disagreed, and the government asked the Supreme Court to reverse the decision.

The Court did not do so. While noting that there were indeed some exceptions to the requirement that the government obtain a warrant before conducting a search, there were only a few of these and they generally existed to protect the life of law enforcement officers. Nor did the language of the act support the government's claim. The act only noted that it did not restrict the president's existing powers; the Court found that these did not include the ability to order a warrantless search, even in issues of national security. The Court had faith that the judges who were asked to grant warrants in these cases would take the national security issues into consideration when deciding whether or not to grant the warrant. The Court therefore reaffirmed the decision of the district court.

ELECTRONIC SURVEILLANCE IN A POST-9/11 AMERICA

In the first decades of the twenty-first century, the power the U.S. government has to monitor the activities and communications of its citizens has expanded greatly beyond mere search warrants and wiretaps. In the wake of the terrorist attacks of September 11, 2001, the U.S. government, under President George W. Bush, gained new powers to monitor the activities and communications of its citizens, including the ability to listen in on phone conversations, monitor private e-mail and other Internet activity, and even track library loans and bookstore purchases. This was largely achieved through the passage of the USA PATRIOT Act. The government retained and continued to utilize these powers under the succeeding administration of President Barack Obama.

State intelligence agencies such as the CIA, the FBI, and the National Security Administration (NSA) are spending millions of dollars on data-mining firms that offer information on all computer users, including the searches they engage in, the things they buy, the e-mails and blogs they write, and the pictures they post. Trusted Internet companies like Google are sharing user information with state agencies like the NSA. The NSA actively monitors a large volume of Americans' private telephone calls and e-mail messages without court warrants.

The federal government is seeking to expand these surveillance powers even further. It wants new regulations for the Internet that will give federal officials a method to wiretap any method of communication. It wants to be able to force Internet providers to redesign electronic communication so each form can be tapped, including e-mails, Skype calls and other Internet voice transmissions, Facebook and Twitter posts, chat room conversations, Flickr photos, YouTube videos, and blog entries. The Justice Department even wants police to have the ability, without getting a warrant, to place a GPS tracking device on an individual's car in order to monitor all of his or her movements.

Some of these powers claimed by the government have been rejected on Fourth Amendment grounds by federal courts of appeals, but that hasn't stopped federal efforts to continue to expand its surveillance of Americans' communications, with or without warrants.

People gather in New York City to protest the federal government's domestic warrantless wiretapping program.

This was not the first time the Court ruled against the federal government in a wiretapping case. In 1974, the Court decided against the administration of President Richard Nixon in *United States v. Giordano*. This case involved authorizations for wiretapping issued by the government but not signed by Attorney General John N. Mitchell or his deputy, but an aide, in violation of the Crime Control Act of 1969, which required the attorney general's signature on such authorizations. Hundreds of warrants were thus invalidated, and the evidence collected by their wiretapping had to be thrown out.

A LOST CELL PHONE STORES EVIDENCE OF A CRIME

In one of the first cases of its kind, the ability to seize text messages without a warrant and use them as evidence of a crime was tested in Aspen, Colorado. On February 18, 2008, Devin Schutter accidentally left his cell phone in a gas station bathroom. It was later retrieved by the gas station clerk, who handed it over to a police officer who arrived several hours later to buy food. The police officer answered several calls on the cell phone and began to suspect it belonged to Schutter, who had a long criminal record in Aspen. The officer then searched through the cell phone's log of text messages and found one that seemed to indicate drug possession and trafficking activities.

Schutter later contacted the police department, asking for his phone back. They refused, instead using the text messages as the basis for a warrant allowing for the search of his mother's home, where they found drugs and drug paraphernalia. Schutter was arrested on charges of dealing cocaine. Schutter's attorney demanded that the charges be dismissed, since the evidence was gathered through a search of the suspect's phone and house that violated constitutional protections against illegal search and seizure.

The Pitkin County District Court judge acknowledged that there was no precedent in Colorado law for the search and seizure of lost cell phones. So he relied upon an earlier precedent that concluded that lost property could be searched and seized and any incriminating evidence used in court if the search is part of a "standardized criteria of procedure." The judge found, however, that the Aspen Police Department had not created any standard criteria for the search and seizure of lost property that came into their possession.

As a result, the judge declared that neither the seized drugs nor the incriminating text messages could be used in court against Schutter. Pitkin County's chief deputy district attorney vowed to appeal the case to Colorado's Supreme Court.

SEARCHING LOCKERS, BACKPACKS, AND POCKETS: THE FOURTH AMENDMENT GOES TO SCHOOL

The question of whether or not the Fourth Amendment is involved in searches of students by school officials has been tested only in the last few years. However, it touches upon some interesting questions about the nature of the Constitution and American government.

In order to maintain a safe environment and to enforce a school's disciplinary rules, school officials must occasionally search students' lockers or even their clothing. However, constitutionally this presents some problems: Is such an operation a "search" in the way the Fourth Amendment means it? If it is, do Fourth Amendment restrictions apply to it, or do school officials enjoy an exemption similar to that enjoyed by the police, who are allowed to perform warrantless searches under some circumstances?

And finally, what are the rights of Americans who are not yet legally "of age"? Are they citizens in the same way an adult is? Do they enjoy the same rights as an adult, or does the government enjoy more power over them and more responsibility for their welfare as well?

The first part of these questions—whether or not the Fourth Amendment applies to students—was not addressed by the Supreme Court until 1985, with their decision in *New Jersey v. T. L. O.* A later decision, *Vernonia School District v. Acton* addressed some of the remaining concerns, although certain areas of this thorny issue still have not been addressed by the Court.

SMOKING IN THE GIRLS' ROOM: *NEW JERSEY V. T. L. O.*

In a New Jersey high school, a teacher found two freshman girls smoking in the bathroom. At this school, smoking was not against the rules, but students who smoked could do so only in certain areas, which did not include the bathroom. The teacher took the girls to the assistant vice principal, Theodore Choplick, who was in charge of discipline. Choplick asked each of the girls if she had been smoking in the bathroom.

The first girl immediately admitted that she had, and Choplick gave her a three-day suspension. However, the second girl, who is known to us only as "T. L. O.," not only did not admit to smoking in the bathroom but also denied having been smoking at

A drug-sniffing dog searches lockers at Austin High School, in Decatur, Alabama.

all. The stage was being set for a confrontation that would eventually reach the Supreme Court.

Choplick then asked for T. L. O.'s purse so that he might search it. This was something he had commonly done as part of his duties at the school. Immediately, he saw some cigarettes in her purse. But that was not all. He saw some cigarette rolling papers, which in his experience meant that the person who had them was using marijuana.

This convinced Choplick to empty out her bag. He found a pipe, a bag containing a substance that smelled like marijuana, and a little book that contained a list of people who owed the girl money.

These factors convinced Choplick that the girl had been selling marijuana. He called her parents and then the police, who arrived and explained the Miranda rights to her. Under the questioning of the police, the girl admitted to selling marijuana, and Choplick gave her ten days' suspension.

However, the local prosecutor then charged T. L. O. with delinquency in juvenile court. Her lawyer fought the juvenile complaint and went to civil court to fight the school suspension, both times using the same argument: her Fourth Amendment rights had been violated by the principal. Therefore, under the exclusionary rule, the evidence against her had to be tossed out.

Up to this point, in the absence of a Supreme Court ruling, three separate theories had evolved about the extent to which school officials were restricted by the Fourth Amendment. The first theory was that the officials were acting in *loco parentis*, a Latin expression meaning "in the place of the parents." In that case, school officials would not be more restrained in searching a student than a parent would.

Others argued that the full force of the Fourth Amendment should apply to school officials. Under this theory, they would need to have probable cause and a warrant in order to search a student, her private space, and her possessions.

The middle position held that while the Fourth Amendment did indeed protect students, the standards should probably be lower than they would be for adults. While this sounded reasonable, some were troubled by the idea that schoolchildren would have less protection than adults accused of a crime have under the law.

The *T. L. O.* case moved slowly through the New Jersey court system, finally reaching the state Supreme Court, which ruled for the moderate position: the Fourth Amendment did indeed apply, but searches needed only to be "reasonable" and did not necessarily need a warrant. However, Choplick's search had not been reasonable. He had had no information indicating the purse contained cigarettes. Possession of cigarettes was not even an offense, and merely possessing cigarettes did not mean that the girl had smoked them in a prohibited place. And finally, emptying out the purse on his desk had not been reasonable in any case. Therefore the evidence was deemed inadmissible.

The state of New Jersey immediately appealed to the U.S. Supreme Court, but, interestingly enough, only on the grounds that the exclusionary rule should not apply to searches conducted by school officials, apparently willing to accept the other restrictions imposed by the state court. The U.S. Supreme Court began to hear arguments on the case in 1984 but soon asked each side to expand its arguments beyond the narrow matter of the exclusionary rule to explore precisely what role the Fourth Amendment had in the public school system.

Under those circumstances, it should have come as no surprise that in the end the Court did not rule about the applicability of the exclusionary rule. Instead, it answered, although this time with much greater finality, the issues the New Jersey court had decided. First, the Court said, the Fourth Amendment did indeed apply to the public school system. However, this did not mean that school officials were expected to learn the ins and outs of probable cause to the same degree required of a police officer. Instead, they would be held to a more general standard of whether or not a search was "reasonable under the circumstances." This meant that the search must be

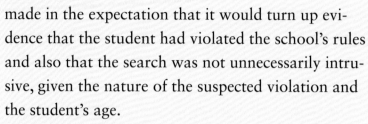

made in the expectation that it would turn up evidence that the student had violated the school's rules and also that the search was not unnecessarily intrusive, given the nature of the suspected violation and the student's age.

The Court then decided that under this standard, Choplick's search had indeed been reasonable in its first goal, finding cigarettes that would tend to disprove T. L. O.'s claim that she had not been smoking. Once the rolling papers were found, Choplick was then justified in expanding his search. The entire search from beginning to end had been reasonable, and thus there was no need to consider whether or not the exclusionary rule would apply.

Ironically, by this point T. L. O. had already graduated high school and was trying to put the historic events of her freshman year in high school behind her.

DRUG TESTING OF STUDENTS: *VERNONIA V. ACTON*

Ten years later, the Court again addressed the question of whether a student's rights were more limited than those of an adult.

The Vernonia, Oregon, school district experienced a rising drug and alcohol problem in the late 1980s. Many of the school district's athletes were the worst offenders, and because of their popularity, other

James Acton *(center, with blue jacket and eyeglasses)*, accompanied by his lawyers, friends, and family, leaves the U.S. Supreme Court after a hearing related to his case. Acton refused to submit to his school's mandatory drug testing of athletes.

students were imitating them and abusing drugs or alcohol as well. The school district began a program of testing all the children in their athletics program for drugs.

The plan called for students who signed up for teams to take a drug test. Then, each week during the season, 10 percent of the athletes on the team, chosen randomly, had to take another drug test. The tests were closely monitored to make sure that the students did not try to "cheat" on them. The results were known only to the district superintendent, and if a student failed, he or she was retested. If he or she failed the second test, the student would be sent to drug counseling or suspended for two seasons.

When a twelve-year-old boy named James Acton decided to try out for the football team, he refused to take the drug test. The school would not let him play without one, though, and Acton's parents sued the school district, claiming that the "blanket" testing violated his Fourth Amendment rights. The case was eventually appealed to the Supreme Court, which issued its decision in 1995.

Acton's basic argument was that the school had no reason to believe that he was taking drugs and therefore mandatory testing was unreasonable. The majority of the Court disagreed, however. While a child certainly had an "expectation of privacy," it

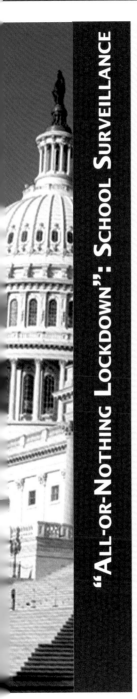

"ALL-OR-NOTHING LOCKDOWN": SCHOOL SURVEILLANCE

"The majority of schools today have adopted an all-or-nothing lockdown mindset that leaves little room for freedom, individuality or due process. Metal detectors, drug-sniffing dogs and pat-down searches have become commonplace, while draconian zero tolerance policies characterize as criminal behavior the most innocuous things, such as students in possession of Alka-Seltzer or a drawing of a soldier. A handful of schools have even gone so far as to require students to drape Radio Frequency Identification (RFID) tags around their necks, which allow school officials to track every single step students take.

As surveillance cameras, metal detectors, police patrols, zero tolerance policies, lockdowns, drug sniffing dogs and strip searches become the norm in elementary, middle and high schools across the nation, America is on a fast track to raising up an Orwellian generation—one populated by compliant citizens accustomed to living in a police state and who march in lockstep to the dictates of the government. And with every school police raid and overzealous punishment that is carried out in the name of school safety, the lesson being imparted is that Americans—especially young people—have no rights at all against the state or the police."

—John W. Whitehead, founder and president of the Rutherford Institute, a civil liberties organization that provides free legal services to people who believe their constitutional and human rights have been violated noted, this expectation was less than what an adult enjoyed. Furthermore, athletes, who used a communal locker room where they would change clothes and shower together, had an even lower standard of privacy. In the face of the compelling crisis of drug use among students, the school district's right to ensure the safety and health of the majority of its members overrode the privacy concerns of individual students. In a sharp dissent, however, Justice Sandra Day O'Connor noted that she could think of no better summary of the Fourth Amendment's protections than James Acton's basic defense—there was no reason to suspect him of anything.

FINDING WHAT THEY WEREN'T LOOKING FOR

In 2009, a case of search and seizure in a California public school was complicated by the fact that school authorities did not find what they were looking for— drugs—but instead found a weapon.

On November 21, 2008, a substitute teacher heard the suspect—known in court documents only as C. M. because he was a minor—discussing a possible drug deal with another student. The substitute teacher alerted the assistant principal of Lakeside's El Capitan High School in San Diego County. C. M. was escorted to the assistant principal's office and was told why he was there and what activity he was suspected of.

The assistant principal then asked permission to search C. M.'s backpack. School officials claim C. M. gave his permission, saying that nothing would be found in it. Nothing was indeed found in the backpack, so the assistant principal asked C. M. to empty his pockets. Again, according to school officials, C. M. complied. When he emptied his pockets, a knife with a 3- or 4-inch (7.6–10 centimeter) blade was discovered.

The district attorney for San Diego County charged C. M. with possession of a knife on school grounds. C. M. and his lawyers sought to have the evidence suppressed, but this motion was denied. C. M. was placed on probation, assigned community service, and forced to pay court fees. C. M. appealed his case to the California Court of Appeals, saying the lower court should have allowed the evidence to be suppressed because his Fourth Amendment rights had been violated. He claims the school lacked reasonable suspicion of criminal activity and any specific facts that would have argued for a search. He also claimed he had not agreed with the assistant principal's request to search the contents of his pockets.

The California Court of Appeals upheld the lower court ruling, pointing out that Fourth Amendment prohibitions on unreasonable searches are more

Christian Balden *(right)* speaks to a campus security officer at Enid High School, in Enid, Oklahoma. Balden is handing out flyers that declare opposition to his school's drug testing policy in which Enid High seniors are required to submit to a drug test before being allowed to participate in extracurricular activities.

"relaxed" in school settings. A court must balance the child's privacy interest with the substantial interest of teachers and administrators in maintaining discipline on school grounds and protecting students from harm, including the presence of drugs, drug trafficking, and weapons on or near school grounds. The legality of a search depends on whether a school official acted reasonably under all of the circumstances of the search. The motivation for the search has to be justified, and the actual scope and conduct of the search must be reasonably related to the circumstances that justified the search in the first place. The appeals court found that the substitute teacher's report on the overheard conversation justified the search and provided reasonable suspicion. The search of the backpack and pants' pockets was further considered reasonable in scope, given that school authorities suspected drug possession.

THE FOURTH AMENDMENT: PROTECTING YOUR RIGHTS

The Fourth Amendment to the Constitution has, in the end, been one of the greatest guarantees of liberty in our country's history. This little amendment, with its somewhat ambiguous wording, has over time expanded its protections, becoming the strongest guarantee of privacy rights in the English-speaking world.

Since before the Revolutionary War, many Americans have believed that a limited government was the best protection they could have for their liberty. Indeed, the Revolution itself was caused in large measure by the attempts of the British government to exert more direct power over the colonists.

Americans have also been suspicious of attempts by the government to intrude upon their privacy and personal space. In a very real sense, liberty, especially American liberty, is the freedom to be "let alone," not to be interfered with by the government.

This basic philosophy is reflected at every level of our Constitution. No other government has a basic document that contains so many rules on what a government may not do. While the federal government is given large and important powers under the

Constitution, these are constantly restricted by the language of the document and checked by the structure of the government itself, which was carefully designed so that each branch balances out the others.

A democracy's greatest test may well be its criminal trials. Nowhere else does the fine balance that must be struck between public and private rights become so clear, so critical, and so crucial. For here is the most powerful test of the basic ideal of American freedom: that no man or woman, in the eyes of the law, is better or worse than another. And, at the same time, the trial system tests whether or not the government's interests are ever to be placed above those of a citizen who is only accused of a crime and who has yet to be proven guilty.

The Founding Fathers had long experience with injustice during the colonial days. They knew that the British general warrants had been terrible tools of oppression, used to ruthlessly attack those who opposed the government, as well as to terrify and cow citizens into complying with unjust laws. Thus, one of the fundamental protections placed into the Bill of Rights was a freedom from these unreasonable searches and seizures.

At the same time, the government must be allowed some ability to look for and acquire evidence of a crime. Society has an important interest in punishing criminals, for if allowing the government too much power can create an injustice by convicting innocent people, just as terrible an injustice occurs when the guilty are allowed to go free. Thus, while the basic concept of the Fourth Amendment is not controversial, almost any application of it is bound to arouse debate, for it is here that we find the most powerful collision between the interests of the state and the interests of a citizen.

In its rulings on the Fourth Amendment, the Court has charted the expanding and changing vision of American liberty. At first the amendment was seen as a protection of property rights, the property rights that were so dear to the Founders and whose violation was another major cause of the Revolution. Yet, just as over time the vision of the Bill of Rights has been expanded, from merely a description of what the federal government must not do against an individual to a positive assertion of the basic freedoms possessed by everyone in the United States that cannot be breached by any government, so has the Fourth Amendment's interpretation changed. A new right, the right to privacy, has grown out of it, and intrusions into a person's privacy, not seizures of his property, are now seen as its main protection.

Over the years, the Court has continued to expand the Fourth Amendment's protections, adopting the doctrine of the exclusionary rule to make inadmissible any evidence seized in violation of the amendment's protections. This controversial rule, as noted previously, is almost unique to American justice, yet such is the standard of liberty demanded by the Constitution, or so the members of the Supreme Court have decided.

Likewise, deciding exactly when the public interest demands that the Fourth Amendment's protections be overridden has caused no end of controversy. Each time, the Court has had to weigh the question of the greater injustice: respecting privacy rights and allowing someone who may be guilty to go free or intruding upon privacy in order to find compelling proof of a crime. It is no wonder, then, that so many times Fourth Amendment rulings have been reversed by later Courts, who found that the previous standards did not fit with more recent conceptions of liberty. Yet this process, as imperfect as it may seem, has preserved the Constitution and the Bill of Rights as living, breathing documents that continue to define not only what it is to be an American but what it is to be free.

PREAMBLE TO THE CONSTITUTION

We the People of the United States, in order to form a more perfect Union, establish Justice, insure domestic Tranquility, provide for the common defense, promote the general Welfare, and secure the Blessings of Liberty to ourselves and our Posterity, do ordain and establish this Constitution for the United States of America.

On September 25, 1789, Congress transmitted to the state legislatures twelve proposed amendments, two of which, having to do with congressional representation and congressional pay, were not adopted. The remaining ten amendments became the Bill of Rights.

THE BILL OF RIGHTS

Amendment I

Congress shall make no law respecting an establishment of religion, or prohibiting the free exercise thereof; or abridging the freedom of speech, or of the press; or the right of the people peaceably to assemble, and to petition the Government for a redress of grievances.

Amendment II

A well regulated Militia, being necessary to the security of a free State, the right of the people to keep and bear Arms, shall not be infringed.

Amendment III

No Soldier shall, in time of peace be quartered in any house, without the consent of the Owner, nor in time of war, but in a manner to be prescribed by law.

Amendment IV

The right of the people to be secure in their persons, houses, papers, and effects, against unreasonable searches and seizures, shall not be violated, and no Warrants shall issue, but upon probable cause, supported by Oath or affirmation, and particularly describing the place to be searched, and the persons or things to be seized.

Amendment V

No person shall be held to answer for a capital, or otherwise infamous crime, unless on a presentment or indictment of a Grand Jury, except in cases arising in the land or naval forces, or in the Militia, when in actual service in time of War or public danger; nor

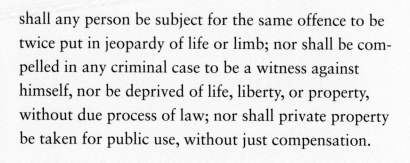

shall any person be subject for the same offence to be twice put in jeopardy of life or limb; nor shall be compelled in any criminal case to be a witness against himself, nor be deprived of life, liberty, or property, without due process of law; nor shall private property be taken for public use, without just compensation.

Amendment VI

In all criminal prosecutions, the accused shall enjoy the right to a speedy and public trial, by an impartial jury of the State and district wherein the crime shall have been committed, which district shall have been previously ascertained by law, and to be informed of the nature and cause of the accusation; to be confronted with the witnesses against him; to have compulsory process for obtaining witnesses in his favor, and to have the Assistance of Counsel for his defense.

Amendment VII

In Suits at common law, where the value in controversy shall exceed twenty dollars, the right of trial by jury shall be preserved, and no fact tried by a jury, shall be otherwise reexamined in any Court of the United States, than according to the rules of the common law.

Amendment VIII

Excessive bail shall not be required, nor excessive fines imposed, nor cruel and unusual punishments inflicted.

Amendment IX

The enumeration in the Constitution, of certain rights, shall not be construed to deny or disparage others retained by the people.

Amendment X

The powers not delegated to the United States by the Constitution, nor prohibited by it to the States, are reserved to the States respectively, or to the people.

appeal To ask a higher court to review the decision in a case and change it.

bill of attainder A law that declares a person guilty of a crime without giving him or her a trial and imposes a sentence. Specifically forbidden in the United States by the Constitution.

checks and balances Fundamental principle behind the construction of the U.S. government. Each branch of government has certain powers granted to it, but the other branches have the power to prevent other branches from abusing their power.

conviction Decision by a jury (or a judge) that a person is guilty of the crime that he or she has been charged with.

counsel A lawyer who assists a person in his or her defense.

defendant In criminal cases, the person who has been indicted for a crime.

evidence Any information that relates to whether or not a person has committed a crime. Evidence may be physical, such as blood samples, or consist of the testimony of witnesses or the opinion of experts about other evidence in the trial.

ex post facto Latin for "after the fact." In constitutional studies, writing a law that punishes a person for an action that was not a crime when it was taken; forbidden by the Constitution.

incorporation In constitutional studies, the expansion of the rights guaranteed by the Bill of Rights to apply to actions taken by the states, not just the federal government. When this occurs, the right is said to have been "incorporated against the states."

jurisdiction The power of a court to hear a specific case. Courts are limited to the kinds of cases they can hear by the laws of their government.

overturn To change the decision of a lower court or a precedent.

probable cause Reasonable belief, based on the evidence presented, that a person has committed a crime; necessary in order to obtain a warrant or indictment.

reverse To change the ruling of a lower court or a precedent to its opposite decision.

suspect A person believed to have committed a crime but who has not yet been indicted.

testimony The statements of a witness during a trial.

warrant A document, issued by a judge or other magistrate, authorizing the arrest of a person or the search of a specific area for evidence of a crime; the warrant must include a specific charge or charges, and probable cause that the person has committed the crime must be shown to the magistrate.

writ of certiorari Special order issued by the Supreme Court granting an appeal to it.

American Civil Liberties Union (ACLU)

125 Broad Street, 18th Floor

New York NY 10004

(212) 549-2500

Web site: http://www.aclu.org

The ACLU views itself as the nation's guardian of liberty, working daily in courts, legislatures, and communities to defend and preserve the individual rights and liberties that the Constitution and laws of the United States guarantee everyone in this country. These rights include free speech, freedom of the press, freedom of association and assembly, freedom of religion, freedom from discrimination, the right to due process, and the right to privacy.

American Law Institute

4025 Chestnut Street

Philadelphia, PA 19104

(215) 243-1600

Web site: http://www.ali.org

The American Law Institute is the leading independent organization in the United States producing scholarly work to clarify, modernize, and otherwise improve the law. The institute (made up of four thousand lawyers, judges, and law professors of the highest qualifications) drafts, discusses, revises, and publishes Restatements of the Law, model statutes, and principles of law that are enormously influential in the courts and legislatures, as well as in legal scholarship and education.

Center for Constitutional Rights (CCR)

666 Broadway, 7th Floor

New York, NY 10012

(212) 614-6464

Web site: http://ccrjustice.org

The Center for Constitutional Rights (CCR) is dedicated to advancing and protecting the rights guaranteed by the U.S. Constitution and the Universal Declaration of Human Rights. Founded in 1966 by attorneys who represented civil rights movements in the South, CCR is a nonprofit legal and educational organization committed to the creative use of law as a positive force for social change.

Center for Democracy and Technology (CDT)

1634 I Street NW, Suite 1100

Washington, DC 20006

(202) 637-9800

Web site: http://www.cdt.org

The Center for Democracy and Technology (CDT) is a nonprofit public interest organization working to keep the Internet open, innovative, and free. As a civil liberties group with expertise in law, technology, and policy, CDT works to enhance free expression and privacy in communication technologies by finding practical and innovative solutions to public policy challenges while protecting civil liberties.

Legal Aid Society

199 Water Street

New York, NY 10038

(212) 577-3346

Web site: http://www.legal-aid.org/en/las/aboutus.aspx

The Legal Aid Society is the nation's oldest and largest provider of legal services to those who cannot afford to hire a lawyer.

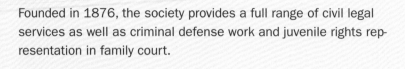

Founded in 1876, the society provides a full range of civil legal services as well as criminal defense work and juvenile rights representation in family court.

People for the American Way

2000 M Street NE, Suite 400
Washington, DC 20036
(202) 467-4999
Web site: http://www.pfaw.org

People for the American Way is dedicated to making the promise of America real for every American, in part by working to insure equality, freedom of speech, freedom of religion, the right to seek justice in a court of law, and the right to cast a vote that counts. Its mission is to promote and maintain a vibrantly diverse democratic society in which everyone is treated equally under the law, given the freedom and opportunity to pursue their dreams, and encouraged to participate in the nation's civic and political life. Its vision of America is of a nation and a people that respect diversity, nurture creativity, and combat hatred and bigotry.

Supreme Court of the United States

1 First Street NE
Washington, DC 20543
(202) 479-3000
Web site: http://www.supremecourt.gov

The Supreme Court of the United States is the highest judicial body in the United States and leads the federal judiciary. It consists of the chief justice of the United States and eight associate justices, who are nominated by the president and confirmed by a majority vote of the Senate. Once appointed, justices effectively have life tenure, which terminates only upon death, resignation, retirement, or conviction on impeachment. The Court meets in Washington, D.C., in the United States Supreme Court Building. The Supreme Court primarily hears appeals of lower court decisions.

WEB SITES

Due to the changing nature of Internet links, Rosen Publishing has developed an online list of Web sites related to the subject of this book. This site is updated regularly. Please use this link to access the list:

http://www.rosenlinks.com/pfcd/sear

Clancy, Thomas K. *The Fourth Amendment: Its History and Interpretation*. Durham, NC: Carolina Academic Press, 2008.

Cuddihy, William J. *The Fourth Amendment: Origins and Original Meaning, 602–1791*. New York, NY: Oxford University Press, 2009.

Fradin, Dennis Brindell. *The Bill of Rights* (Turning Points in U.S. History). Tarrytown, NY: Marshall Cavendish Children's Books, 2008.

Galiano, Dean. *The Fourth Amendment: Unreasonable Search and Seizure*. New York, NY: Rosen Central, 2011.

Isaacs, Sally Senzell. *Understanding the Bill of Rights* (Documenting Early America). New York, NY: Crabtree Publishing Co., 2008.

Leavitt, Amie J. *The Bill of Rights in Translation: What It Really Means*. Mankato, MN: Capstone Press, 2008.

Lee, Cynthia. *Searches and Seizures: The Fourth Amendment: Its Constitutional History and Contemporary Debate*. Amherst, NY: Prometheus Books, 2010.

McInnis, Thomas N. *The Evolution of the Fourth Amendment*. Lanham, MD: Lexington Books, 2009.

Newman, Bruce A. *Against That "Powerful Engine of Despotism": The Fourth Amendment and General Warrants at the Founding and Today*. Lanham, MD: University Press of America, 2006.

Slobogin, Christopher. *Privacy at Risk: The New Government Surveillance and the Fourth Amendment.* Chicago, IL: University of Chicago Press, 2007.

Smith, Richard E. *Fourth Amendment: The Right to Privacy.* Edina, MN: ABDO & Daughters, 2007.

Sobel, Syl. *The Bill of Rights: Protecting Our Freedom Then and Now.* Hauppauge, NY: Barron's Educational Series, 2008.

Taslitz, Andrew E. *Reconstructing the Fourth Amendment: A History of Search and Seizure, 1789–1868.* New York, NY: NYU Press, 2009.

Taylor-Butler, Christine. *The Bill of Rights.* New York, NY: Children's Press, 2008.

Woody, Robert Henley. *Search and Seizure: The Fourth Amendment for Law Enforcement Officers.* Springfield, IL: Charles C. Thomas Publisher, Ltd., 2006.

Yero, Judith Lloyd. *American Documents: The Bill of Rights.* Des Moines, IA: National Geographic Children's Books, 2006.

ABOUT THE AUTHORS

Brian Carson is a writer in Boston, Massachusetts.

Catherine Ramen is a writer who lives in New York City.

PHOTO CREDITS

Cover, pp. 1, 12, 24, 38, 46, 56, 74, 88, 103, 114, 126 Brian Harkin/Getty Images; p. 4 Don Murray/Getty Images; p. 14 Mario Tama/Getty Images; p. 19 Hulton Archive/Getty Images; p. 20 © The Trustees of the British Museum/Art Resource, NY; p. 27 MPI/Getty Images; pp. 32, 65, 112, 128, 133, 138–139 © AP Images; p. 34 Chip Somodevilla/ Getty Images; p. 39 The Bridgeman Art Library/Getty Images; p. 43 Win McNamee/Getty Images; pp. 48, 69, 78 Robert Nickelsberg/Getty Images; p. 53 © www.istock-photo.com/Deborah Cheramie; p. 58 Craig Hartley/ Bloomberg via Getty Images; p. 62 Mario Villafuerte/Getty Images; p. 75 Chris Hondros/Getty Images; p. 83 Bill Clark/ Roll Call/Getty Images; p. 90 Chris Polk/FilmMagic/Getty Images; pp. 96, 107 Justin Sullivan/Getty Images; p. 100 Robyn Beck/AFP/Getty Images; p. 104 David McNew/Getty Images; p. 115 Tim Boyle/Getty Images; p. 120 Paul J. Richards/AFP/Getty Images; p. 123 showcasepix/Newscom. com; other interior images © www.istockphoto.com.

Photo Researcher: Amy Feinberg